CRUMBLE OR STAND

God bless
Tori Ann
x

CRUMBLE OR STAND

The Power of Forgiveness

My Story
of being abandoned,
rejected, broken-hearted
and left unloved

Toni Ann

Copyright Toni Ann © 2014

Produced in association with

www.wordsbydesign.co.uk

ISBN: 978-1-291-91142-8

British Library Cataloguing in Publication Data
A catalogue record for this book is available from the British Library

Cover illustration © Jenny Whitfield

Unless otherwise indicated, all Scripture quotations taken from the Holy Bible, New
International Version (NIV) © 1973, 1978, 1984 by International Bible Society.
Used by permission of Hodder & Stoughton, a member of the Hodder Headline Group.
"NIV" is a trademark of International Bible Society.

Dedication

I dedicate this book to my three beautiful children.

Each of you is amazing, precious and beautiful.

Thank you for making me smile and laugh every day.

I love you so very much.

Contents

Foreword

When Toni contacted me about her book, I was excited to read it because she has taken up the challenge of telling the world through her book *Crumble or Stand*, about how she handled a traumatic period in her life. I applaud Toni's courage in writing this book, because there are many books out there written about mountain-top moments, but which never share true life stories in the valley.

I started reading this book with curiosity and expectation. I enjoyed it so much that I could not drop it or postpone reading until the next day. I finished reading *Crumble or Stand* at 2.25a.m. True to my expectation, Toni did not hold back, as she opened herself up through 'Crumble or Stand' to encourage, motivate and impact us positively to demonstrate love and compassion, irrespective of what she was going through.

This book touched and blessed me personally because of Toni's commitment to her marriage, family and church. In spite of all the challenges Toni was going through, she demonstrated godly character, love, patience, endurance, forgiveness and compassion. Hence, in this book you will learn, amongst other things, the unconditional love that can only be demonstrated through an abiding walk of faith in Christ; how to get up and continue with your Christian race in order to fulfil your God-ordained destiny, regardless of what you are going through, knowing that God is always with you and for you; and that joy and happiness in life comes from within you (internal), but not what happened to you.

Crumble or Stand is a book that teaches you how to face challenges with fortitude and grace. Toni's attitude to life as explained in this book will encourage you not to give up, not to crumble, but to keep standing, irrespective of life challenges. This book educates us on how to rely on God, forgive and love people unconditionally.

When disasters happen or when hope is dashed and expectations are not fulfilled, one's reactions could manifest themselves in form of self-doubts, discouragement, disappointment and rejection. One may get confused about the validity of a personal relationship with the Lord, and may ask the question: "Why me, Lord?" These thoughts paint a gloomy picture of failure, as if one's dream and pursuit of happiness can't be achieved. But when Toni's marriage broke down, she encouraged herself in the Lord and embraced the unconditional love of Christ which turned her defeat to victory. Toni did not only survive the breakdown of her marriage; she became stronger in faith and love.

The testimonies from Toni's family and friends in this book authenticate her honesty. This book will teach you not to allow storms, challenges, abandonment or rejection to hold you back or crumble you, but to rise up above all storms and keep marching on in Christ Jesus.

Finally this book will teach you how to take hold of God's keys of unconditional love and follow the path of forgiveness and freedom. Toni's journey during her troubled time demonstrates to us that the unconditional love of Christ is more than a change of attitude; it is a dynamic process of a daily walk of fellowship and relationship with Jesus and with people in general.

This practical book *Crumble or Stand* tells the story of a unique Christian woman, Toni, who overcame hopeless situations with love through Christ, and teaches us to embrace love, endurance and forgiveness in our journey of total restoration in Christ.

Dr Elizabeth Omole
Preacher, Lecturer & Entrepreneur (UK)
Author of *Changing your World through Prayer*

An Introduction

Tears poured down my face as I quietly sat in the chair, surrounded by tissues, shaking. My heart was completely broken. It was all a bit surreal. I sobbed. I felt sick.

My eldest daughter ran upstairs to her bedroom quickly. She sat on her window-sill waving. Tears rolled down her face. My two other children stood on the couch and waved furiously out of the window.

They were waving at their Dad. He had spent the last few hours packing his belongings into his car. He opened the driver's side door, got in his car and drove off down the street.

He was their hero, until now. Hearts were broken, smashed to pieces, devastated beyond words. Abruptly, our lives had turned upside down. Everything that was familiar to us lay in ruins at our feet. Our family, destroyed in a heartbeat.

This is my story of when I discovered that my husband was having an affair: the day he closed the front door; the devastation he left behind; and the agonising steps that followed.

The journey has been so incredibly tough, harrowing and full of pain. As I summon the courage to bare my heart and soul to you, tears well in my eyes. Sadly, being deceived and discarded leaves its own trail of scars.

My aim of writing this book is to reach out to those who are broken, hurting, rejected, abandoned and unloved; to say to all men and women who have been the 'victim' of a cruel act, such as adultery, that you are not on your own.

I have had to fight for my integrity, self-respect and confidence on a daily basis. There have been days when I completely crumbled under the weight of the emotional torment and pain. But I never gave up trying.

I live with my three beautiful children in Berkshire, in the United Kingdom. I am not a teacher, or a scholar, nor do I profess to be. I hold no qualifications. I am just me.

I am a Christian and a church leader in my local church. Throughout this book I want to share how God has helped me on my journey. I have used references from the Bible and explained how these have helped me. My prayer is that this book will be a blessing to you in some small way.

Much love,

Toni x

Acknowledgements

First, I must thank God, the Lord Jesus Christ, for showering me with His unending grace, mercy and love from day one. God has taught me that love and forgiveness overrides every emotion; and that standing *is* possible.

Mum and Dad:

Thank you for always being there for us; for your love and support; all those dinners, shopping trips, cups of tea, and laughs together. You are both so amazing. I love you so much.

Nan:

Thank you for the times you sat and listened to me. For the many hours we sat laughing together over a cup of tea. I love you, Nan.

Great-Aunty:

Thank you for your love and support. You are so lovely. I love you.

Mum-in-Law:

Thank you for everything. You are incredible. Thank you for holding my hand. I love you.

Brothers-in-law and Sisters-in-law:

Thank you for always being there for us. You are incredible and I love each of you dearly.

My editor:

Thank you for helping me to bring together all my thoughts, ideas and multitude pages of scribbles and writing, into one book. You have been absolutely inspirational, patient and understanding. Thank you for persevering with me through to the end, I am so grateful.

To my proof-readers (LO, JS, BH, TC, NS, JJ):

Thank you, each of you: for your diligence, wisdom, and unending kindness in being willing to proof-read and re-proof-read this book. You are all so fabulous. Thank you for sharing your ideas and comments, and for helping this book take final shape.

Also to my three children, my Mum & Dad, thank you for reading this book first, and giving it your approval and blessing, and to my Great Aunt and Nan, thank you for your blessings too.

To all my friends and family:

Without each of you, I would have been lost. You have been with me through the good days and the not-so-good ones. Thank you. I love you.

Please note:

My ex-husband has given me permission to write and publish this book, for which I am very grateful.

Chapter 1: The Beginning

Six Months Prior

February 2010

As I was sitting on the bus on the way home from work my heart was so very sad. It was Saturday 6th February 2010. I got off the bus and started walking home up the hill. Dread was sitting in my stomach – the dread of walking into the front door – into the unknown.

What would be waiting for me today? I could feel myself growing weary. My legs seemed heavier than normal as I walked up the steep alleyway towards my house. I sighed. I couldn't muster the energy to go any faster.

I neared the flattened bit of the hill and all of a sudden, I heard the words in my ears, as clearly as someone talking next to me: "Trust in the Lord with all your heart and lean not on your own understanding." It is a passage from the Bible.

I stopped. My heart stopped. The words were so loud, so audible. I looked around me. There was no-one there. The alleyway was empty, everything was unusually quiet. There was a little light, a hazy glimmer from the street lamp at the top. A cold metal handrail was to my left. Leaning, oversized fence panels, interwoven with foliage, towered either side, hemming me in. I wouldn't usually stop here.

At that moment I knew that it was God who was speaking to me. It was God – I knew it was. *Who else could it have been?* Suddenly my whole body seemed to be on high alert.

I turned and glanced at the top of the alley. I was all alone. There was no-one else near me. My heart was beating faster now. My feet were rooted to the spot. All I could think of were the words: "Trust in the Lord with all your heart."

The word 'trust' was like a drumbeat in my brain, repeatedly going around in my mind. It seemed so loud, so audible. I was so aware of it. It overshadowed any fear.

The words from the book of Proverbs were not new to me. I'd read them many times; but now that Scripture was all I could think about.

I must have looked quite strange standing there in the dark. I remember feeling small, insignificant with my cream coat buttoned up and with my scarf and gloves. I was carrying a shopping bag dangling from my right hand, just standing there, in the darkness … all alone.

Still thinking about those words, I began to walk to the top of the alleyway. It all seemed so surreal.

I turned the corner, looked across the street at my front door and took a few deep breaths. The sadness had returned to the pit of my stomach. Just glancing at the front door made me feel really nervous.

I knew in that moment that I didn't want to face opening the front door. I didn't want to. I couldn't face it. I squeezed my eyes shut and sighed.

I walked across the road and up the two steps. Reaching out my hand to open the door, I let my fingers rest on the metal handle and swallowed. I didn't want to go in. I hesitated for a second, clasped the handle downwards and opened the door with a heavy heart.

"Trust in the Lord with all your heart and lean not on your own understanding" was the passage from the Bible, still swimming around my head.

God had spoken to me back there in the alleyway! I was so sure of it.

The first time I heard God's voice was a number of years ago.

I had just dropped my daughter off at her nursery. My husband was visiting his brother abroad. Only two streets away, I approached a roundabout which was very busy. There was a big lorry behind me. I had my head turned sharply to the right, watching for an opportunity to cross, when suddenly my car was shunted forward. SMASH! My head was flung first forwards and then backwards as glass shattered everywhere.

By the evening, it became more and more difficult to move my neck. I knew there was something seriously wrong.

The next two years were consumed with doctor's appointments and excruciating daily pain.

One day I was lying on the 'roller-bed' at the osteopath's surgery where I had become a frequent visitor. So far, I had visited him more than seventy times and had yet to reach the end of my treatment.

I remember that particular day vividly. I was still suffering immensely and each day I was consumed by physical agony. Life was so limited. There was no freedom to be myself and do the things that I enjoyed.

The osteopath was bustling about, setting the timer and talking to me constantly. He was a lovely, kind, elderly gentleman, always pleasant and cheerful. He put the timer on and then walked across the room towards the door.

"I'll leave you here and I will be back at the end," he said as he flicked the light switch off and walked out of the room, closing the door behind him. Immediately, soft music enveloped the room as I closed my eyes.

A few minutes later I heard someone say, "You don't need to be here any more."

"What?" I thought, startled. My eyes opened wide. I struggled onto my elbows and looked around the room. No-one was there. The osteopath had left the room. The door was still closed.

Again, the same soft voice said, "You don't need to be here any more."

"WHAT?" I was quite panicked by now. *Don't need to be here? What?* I lay down on the bed again. I lay very still. *What did that mean?*

"Is that you, God?" I muttered under my breath. I stared at the white metal blinds above the bed. "But I like coming here!" I said aloud.

I closed my mouth and stopped talking. *This is ridiculous*, I thought.

I then muttered again, "If that's you, God, then you are going to have to do something!"

I was almost arguing. I still felt in pain. The pain hadn't gone away.

"OK, God," I said. "If I don't have to come here any more, then you need to do something, and I won't come here any more."

I was not convinced; not convinced at all!

Then things all seemed to happen very suddenly. DING! The timer bell went off, the roller-bed came to a halt, the door flung open, and in marched the osteopath carrying my notes. With rising panic, I looked at him wondering, *what do I do now?*

As he walked up to me, he quickly put my notes at the end of the bed and helped me down, in quite a determined fashion.

"Well, Toni," he said, "I don't think we need to see you now for another six months, when it will be time for an MOT."

I stared at him. My eyes wide. I was astounded. I wanted to scream at him, "GOD'S HEALED ME!" But I was speechless and too frightened that he would think I had gone completely mad! I wanted to hug him. I wanted to jump up and down on the spot. But I didn't. Instead, I said "Thank you," quickly turned and gathered my coat and bag.

My car was parked just outside the entrance. I climbed in. As I turned the key in the ignition, I gripped the steering wheel with both hands and closed my eyes.

Still smiling, I said aloud, "God, you are so AMAZING!"

I never went back. I completely believed that God had healed my back.

That is why, standing in the alleyway, some years later, I was certain that the voice I had heard was God's voice.

I hung up my coat on the coat hook inside the doorway. I took off my scarf and placed it in the bag which was overflowing with wintry accessories. I took off my shoes and walked into the lounge. Dread, anticipation, fear and anxiety were filling my whole being.

This was no place to announce that I believed that God had just spoken to me moments before. I didn't say anything about it; instead I tried to appear normal. This was difficult as the scripture was still buzzing around my head, especially the words: "and lean not on your own understanding." *What did that really mean?* I didn't understand what was going on. I felt terribly uncomfortable and nervous in my own home, which was not right. It was meant to be my place of safety, but instead of feeling safe, I felt very afraid; trapped in a bubble of anxiety.

If only I had known what was to follow in the next few days. I would have screamed at the top of my voice in horror.

When It All Began – Summer 2009

Six months before God spoke to me in the alleyway we were on holiday in the Lake District. As we sat all together eating breakfast, looking out on the most beautiful view of Lake Windermere, I looked across the table at my husband. That was the very day, the very moment I saw it.

I don't know how to describe it really, but I saw there was something different about him. He looked the same; he was chatting to the children as normal, but as I looked at him I saw him as being 'distant'. I'm struggling to find the right words, but I knew in my heart something was very wrong.

There was a lost expression in his eyes. I asked him if he was alright. He replied that he was fine. As the week progressed though, it was obvious there was something going on with him – it frightened me a little. He wouldn't talk to me about it. Instead he just said he was tired from work.

But it kept niggling at me all week. He was aloof. We all liked walking in the hills and would set out for a day's walking as normal, but as the days progressed I noticed little things – he didn't hold my hand, or walk next to me. Instead he walked ahead with two of the children and left me and one of our daughters to trail behind. We had always kissed at every kissing gate for years on our walks. But not this week. Even the children began to comment.

At the time I could only say that it was very odd behaviour. It wasn't anything really major so that I felt it was not worth making a fuss about. I persuaded myself that it was due to his promotion and the extra responsibilities at work.

Over the next few weeks he started to go out in the evenings more than usual. A couple of times he was late home for dinner. As the autumn months went by, it became more and more frequent, so much so, that in November and December he hardly ate at all with me and the children.

During this time his phone would be going off constantly and he would always be reading his messages or texting. When I asked him who it was, he would become really defensive and quite annoyed with me for asking.

He started to become secretive as well. He would reply to a text message, then slip the phone back into his pocket without a word. And the texts were becoming more and more frequent.

It was so out of character for him to behave in this way.

I had met him twenty years earlier, in 1990. I had been fortunate to find a temporary job as a typist near Wargrave. I remember that first day. As I looked up from my desk, the first thing I noticed was his eyes. They were a rich deep blue and when he smiled, little creased lines appeared next to each one. He seemed quite shy and softly spoken. I thought he was very handsome.

Our first date did not go so well. He took me to a football match. It was typical winter weather – cold, raining and wet. We were in the stands outside and it was freezing. I didn't even like football! He introduced me to one of his brothers. That did not go well either; he made fun of the hat I was wearing. I still remember that; and the hat! It was navy blue with a little rim that scooped upwards, much like the straw hat I had to wear as part of my school uniform.

Despite our rocky start, I fell head over heels in love with him, even though we were completely different characters. I was small; he was tall. I was bubbly and talkative; he was quiet. I was a worrier; he was very relaxed and 'chilled out'. He liked football, I liked dancing. We were complete opposites. But somewhere in all of that we were 'right' for each other.

After seven months we got engaged. It came as a shock to both our families. One, we were 'too young', and two, it was 'too soon'. Mum and Dad held an engagement party for us in their garden. It was a gorgeous June day. The sun was shining and the lawn was full of family and friends. He was nineteen years old and I was 21.

Eighteen months later, a week before my twenty-third birthday, we were married. The church where we got married was a beautiful, old building, with traditional pews and stunning stained-glass windows. It had an oversized archway over the front door, which was a perfect backdrop for photographs. It was a very cold day, overcast and devoid of sunlight.

As I walked down the aisle I could not help but smile. He looked amazing. He was dressed in a navy suit, with a colourful paisley waistcoat peeping out from under his jacket. A white flower was pinned to the buttonhole on his jacket. His single-breasted suit jacket was neatly buttoned and pressed. His shoes shone. His three brothers, standing by his side, were all dressed in the same suits. Together, they looked fantastic.

He was smiling back at me as I took each step closer to the altar. When I looked into his eyes, butterflies that had been fluttering around in my stomach all morning disappeared.

Following the ceremony we went into a little side room to sign the register. When we walked out of the door and down the aisle together, everybody stood up. We started giggling together as our choice of music began. Everybody was momentarily silent before erupting into surprised laughter and applause. Our choice of music was rather unusual. It was the music to Match of the Day. It was great fun to be walking out of the church to Match of the Day!

I can't remember when and how we decided on that music, but I have never regretted it. Just thinking about it makes me smile. We hadn't told anyone about that part of the ceremony and instead had left it as a surprise. It was most certainly a surprise which caused much chuckling afterwards.

I never thought I would be marrying an Englishman as I had lived in New Zealand most of my life. I had returned to the UK for my 21st birthday and I didn't anticipate remaining here.

When I think back to my life there in New Zealand I am always reminded of the challenges that I faced as a child.

I was born with asthma. I was the girl in the classroom that everyone knew had asthma. It seemed to dominate my early childhood. I was limited to what I could do, but even as a young child I was very determined. I was not going to let it beat me! I was determined to beat it!

I wanted desperately to be like everybody else. I wanted to run, skip, hop and play just like everybody else. I did all that I could do, even though I faced daily limitations.

I remember the day that I refused to quit. Each year our whole Primary School took part in a running competition. We had to run around the streets surrounding the school.

I can see myself now. The memory is so clear:

> I was running, dressed in my school colour: blue. Blue shorts, white tee-shirt and a blue netball top. A boy from my class was running next to me. I had my blue inhaler in my right hand, and my left hand was tightly clenched.
>
> I was tired. I was more than tired. But I was going to finish!
>
> I felt the adrenaline surging through my body. I was drenched in sweat. I couldn't talk to my running companion even if I tried. I couldn't breathe and talk at the same time. He kept talking and I kept puffing. I was breathing hard.
>
> I was approaching the entrance to the tunnel. It was a major tunnel for the cars to pass through. I was nearly there. I had almost made it. I kept going. I kept thinking; why is this boy running next to me, when he can run much faster?
>
> I made it to the tunnel. There was a small path that ran along the side with an enclosed metal chain fence.
>
> I kept going. It was hard. Cars were zooming past. It was dusty and dirty. I had never made it through here. I kept going. I made it through the tunnel. I kept going. I didn't stop, not once. We came out of the tunnel and ran down the hill and round the corner. The school gate was so close! I was doing it; I was going to make it!
>
> We turned into the school drive and ran up the hill. I had done it! I couldn't believe it! I was jumping for joy!
>
> My Mum came to pick me up from school that day. I ran up to her, jumped into her arms shouting, "I done it! I done it! I done it!"

Even when we mention it now, thirty years on, my Mum beams at the memory.

After many, failed attempts, I had finished the course. I didn't know it then but the boy running next to me was there to protect me and encourage me just in case I collapsed with an asthma attack.

That day changed my life. I was on top of the world! I had defied all the odds! I had made it! For the rest of the children it was an ordinary race but for me it was such an achievement. To see everybody finishing the race every year, and me failing, was so disheartening. I was determined to do it! From that day, I was determined to do everything! Including absolutely every sport I could take up.

I am so thankful to my parents for their encouragement. They always encouraged me and told me I could do anything I put my mind to.

Head-first down the hill on my skateboard I was constantly risking my life. Shin pads, elbow pads or helmets were not compulsory then!

My Dad didn't help matters. He not only bought me my first skateboard, but he bought me my first chopper bike too. I couldn't even touch the ground with the tips of my toes. The bike was made for a boy really. It wasn't pink or girly, but blue, with a little flag on the back which stuck high into the air. In order to stop, I had to pull on my brakes really hard and jump off sideways.

In Primary School I played in the netball, tennis and swimming teams. My friend and I also joined a local marching band. We spent hours and hours practising. I used to wear an orange and white costume, with a big bushy hat. It was just like the hat the guards wear outside Buckingham Palace; except mine was orange! My boots were knee-high white lace-ups and I loved them. I spent hours polishing them. I would march up and down the back garden path, practising my moves for hours.

Even when I went to Secondary School I carried on playing sports. I was quite competitive at netball. My position was centre as I was always the smallest.

My friend and I used to do every sporting activity. We went swimming, trampolining, gymnastics and roller-skating whenever we could.

There was an, empty, abandoned, outdoor roller-skating rink near my Nan and Granddad's house. We would zoom down the hill on our bikes, roller-skates dangling over the handlebars, and head for the rink. It was so much fun. There was an indoor rink too, on the other side of the bay. That was where all the real action was. We spent nearly every Saturday skating there.

Just walking in, with the music and disco ball lights playing and spinning, felt so exciting. We were twelve years old. The rink was old, smelly and dusty. There were no seats, only long old wooden step benches to one side. But we all loved it and lots of us met there, all different ages.

We were just a group of kids who loved to roller-skate, but it soon became more than just skating – it was a competition. Everyone wanted to be better than the next one so we all quickly learned to skate. We learned to skate fast, forwards, backwards, in circles, followed by screeching stops. Sometimes there were tumbles, but once you have hit the hard rink at full force, you do your best to avoid it again.

The best part was jumping over people. We would each take it in turn to lie down on our backs on the rink. First one, then two, then three, all the way up to five people, our bodies all squished up close together.

The person skating would skate around the rink once then, as they rounded the corner and straightened up, they would go as fast as they could, heading towards the prone bodies when they would jump as far as they could. The plan would be to jump without causing injury either to themselves or to the people being jumped over! That was the challenge! Jumping one or two people was easy, but you needed real skill to jump over five people!

I was only petite, but I was good; in fact, I was more than good! And I reached the point where I could jump over five people. Roller-skating was one of my key talents. I had the gear too. Mum and Nan sewed for hours. I would produce patterns and material and ask them to make tops for me. These weren't ordinary tops they were shiny blue, long-sleeved, silky shirts with two pockets at the front. Running under each arm and across the back was a row of tassels. I felt so 'cool' when I would skate around the rink in those tops. As I held my arms out the tassels would look amazing. I was the only one wearing them. They may not have been fashionable but they were stunning!!

I have always been a very sociable person. I think it stems from being an only child. My best friend and I were like sisters. As we went through Secondary School together we made friends with three other girls. The five of us stuck together like glue. I think this is where I developed my passion for family and friends. They were so important to me.

I missed them terribly when I came to live in the UK. They were my best friends. I was extremely homesick for everything for a long time but then I met my husband and my life took a new direction.

Twenty years later, following that holiday in the Lake District, I knew things weren't the same as before. That same fun-loving husband had changed. He grew quieter and more distant. He had been cleverly funny and always had a way of making me laugh. His smile would light up a room. When I looked into his eyes my heart would melt. I loved and trusted him. But something was different; something had changed.

He had always been an amazing Dad to our children. He had always spent time with them. He would take them to the park, or on trips to see different places and sights. When he would come home from work, he would always come in with a smile on his face. We would all sit down at the table and have dinner together as a family. It was a time for us to talk about the adventures of our day. We would go around the table and each share for five minutes before having pudding, cups of tea and more chatter. It was our tradition.

After dinner he would help the children with their homework; play football in the back garden or play games on the computer. He would let our girls put his hair up in hair bands or paint his nails whilst he was watching sport on the television. Nothing was too much trouble for him. He was their hero. He was their Dad. He seemed to have endless time for them.

We always looked forward to him walking through the front door. The atmosphere in the house would change to sheer excitement and joy when he came home. There was so much laughter in the house. He was a natural comedian, speaking in silly voices and often telling jokes that would have us in stitches. He never got upset, angry or cross at anyone; it wasn't in his nature. He was the kindest, gentlest, most fun-loving and genuine person I knew.

He was a wonderful husband too. For the last few years he had taken a week off work around February time. We would drop the children off at school and then we would go to the cinema, or drive to a country pub for lunch, or go shopping together, or go for a walk in the country and then go to collect the children from school.

He was the piece of the jigsaw that made our family complete. Everyone loved him. Our family and friends loved him. He was respected by everyone.

But things were changing.

October 2009

I will never forget that day. The children were at school, and I was at home in the kitchen. As I was drying the dishes I was praying, seeking answers, asking God what was wrong. Suddenly, the word 'infidelity' came into my thoughts. It was as clear as a bell. I stopped what I was doing. I went straight to the dictionary. I knew what it meant, but I just wanted to be sure. It said 'sexual unfaithfulness to one's wife, husband …' I just froze.

I stood there looking at the words on the page. I started to cry. I just couldn't believe it. Not my husband! Not the person I treasured most in the entire world – it just couldn't be possible! I stood paralyzed. Then I started to doubt myself – maybe it wasn't God speaking to me, maybe I had got it all wrong.

Then the words that one of my closest friends had said to me in confidence came flooding into my mind. She herself had been wary to share it with me as it posed so many questions. That had been seven months earlier in March 2009.

She'd had a dream. It was about my husband and me. My friend described the dream like this:

> In the dream I came to your front door. You passed by me going
> out of the door, holding a Bible. Then your husband also walked
> past me, out of your house with another woman.

I closed the dictionary. My heart was racing. It couldn't be true! Not my husband! That was too much to believe! It played on my mind for quite a few days. I walked around with a huge fear in my heart. I simply couldn't believe it. So I tried my best to put it out of my mind, dismissing it. I did consider confronting him about it, but it was only a brief thought and looking back, I think it was because I was afraid it would make things worse. So I swept it all under the carpet.

It was a wrong decision. If only I had said, "God said to me today the word 'infidelity' – are you having an affair?" If only I had been brave enough to face it! If only I had opened my eyes to what was going on around me! *If only* I had confronted him. Would things have turned out differently? Would the pain have been less? Maybe he would have been remorseful and willing to work things out with me? Maybe?

But I could literally wear myself out thinking about all the *'If onlys'*. God had warned me but I had refused to listen. God tried to tell me but I had refused to see it. I'd had a window of opportunity to do something, but I chose not to act.

I do so regret not listening to God for, while I was sweeping it under the carpet, things were about to get much, much worse.

November 2009

> *Psalm 86:1-2*
> *Hear, O Lord, and answer me, for I am poor and needy. Guard my life, for I am devoted to you. You are my God; save your servant who trusts in you.*

One morning I woke very early when everyone was still sleeping. I went into the bathroom. His phone was lying on the side as usual. I picked it up and turned it on. I was really nervous. I had never looked at his phone 'in secret' before. I opened the inbox: 'Empty.' I opened the sent box: 'Empty.' My heart started pounding inside my chest. *How weird is that? No messages in or out!*

My phone is the opposite – I delete messages when the boxes are too full! I felt a surge of worry. I scrolled down through his contacts. I knew everyone … except one lady's name. She was listed three times – home, mobile and another mobile. I panicked! I felt sick! I was tempted to write down the numbers but I didn't. I turned off the phone and got ready for work.

A few hours later I was sitting in the lounge. I didn't know what to do. Then he appeared.

"Who is … (the lady's name)?" I asked.

His reaction was unexpected. He looked at me, shocked and angry.

"You've been looking at my phone!" he shouted. "She's only a work colleague." Then: "How dare you look at my phone! Is nothing private?" Seething, he strode into the kitchen. I still sat in the chair. I didn't shout back. I was too stunned. I was too overwhelmed. It was so unlike him.

I had to go to work in a few minutes. *What should I do?*

He didn't come out of the kitchen for a few minutes. I could hear him banging about in there. I didn't know what was happening.

He was furious with me. As he emerged from the kitchen, he didn't speak to me. Instead he pursed his lips together in anger and glared at me sitting in the lounge. I felt cold to my stomach.

I *had* to go to work and I couldn't be late. I felt in shock. He hadn't admitted anything. He had reacted so badly that I felt guilty. I really did feel guilty. What had I done? Who was she? Was she really only a work colleague? It didn't seem right that her number was listed three times.

What was I thinking? Should I have written down the telephone number and called it myself? I didn't know what to think. My mind was in chaos.

When I got to work I felt worse. What did this mean? What will he say when I get home? Why did I say anything at all? It's all my fault!

I was consumed by guilt, fear and trepidation.

From that evening my husband began hiding his phone when he went to bed. It was no longer on the bathroom side each morning.

His behaviour began to change in all sorts of ways. He became very irritable, fidgety, on edge, grumpy and short-tempered. He came home later and later until he stopped spending any time with the children at all in the evenings. He was constantly distracted.

In between this, there was the computer. He would always be on it late at night for ages before he came up to bed.

Looking back, I can see how obvious it all appeared. I almost want to scream to myself: "All the signs were there! He was having an affair!"

The only excuse for my complete and utter naïvety was that I loved him with all my heart. I trusted him. He was the love of my life and had been for seventeen years. Stupidly, I believed him when he said he was 'working late'.

Then he started texting me, saying things like: "Going to London tonight to see a film, is that OK?" Well, what could I say? I could hardly say, "No – you can't go!" He had always gone out with his mates from work and it had never been an issue. But now his messages were very different, cold almost. I was too scared to say, "Actually no! It isn't alright."

Then he would walk into the house at three in the morning. Hindsight is a great gift! Now I can see clearly! But it was so dreadful! I don't know which was worse – him treating me like a doormat – or me acting like one! Back then, I was completely confused, and blindly trusting.

The texts came on an almost daily basis. The excuses flooded in as to why he was going to be late: "Missed the bus"; "On my way home now"; "Worked late…"

A few weeks before my birthday I was very sick with the 'flu. After a couple of days I phoned my doctor's surgery. The answerphone message said something like, "If you think you have swine 'flu please contact …" Well, I didn't know what I had but it was the worst kind of 'flu I had ever experienced. I phoned the swine 'flu helpline, answered their questions, and according to the person on the other end of the line, I had swine 'flu! Tablets for me would be ready for someone to collect later that day.

I phoned my husband at work. He said he would collect the medicine. Around 4.30pm I was still upstairs in bed. I heard him come in the door. He came upstairs and handed me my medicine. He said that he had bought pizza and chips for the children and explained to our daughter, then aged eleven, how to cook everything.

Amazingly, he then announced that he was going to London. I was completely astounded! I was so very sick and he was going out! He had told me about the event previously, but I couldn't believe he would actually leave me while I was obviously so very ill!

I needed him! The children needed him. I had been poorly for a couple of days. I had no energy, my head was pounding and I had a temperature. It felt like the worst migraine, mixed together with all symptoms of 'flu. But more than that, I couldn't believe that he would leave our eleven-year-old in charge of dinner. *What if she burned herself?* I couldn't even lift my head off the pillow! I felt helpless, powerless, incapable and weak.

My daughter was very confident at baking. She had been baking cakes since she was nine without my help. She was capable of using the oven but she had never cooked dinner before by herself, even if it was only pizza and chips. I was so grateful to God for keeping the children safe that night.

I couldn't sleep or rest. I was so worried. I called his mobile. It was turned off. Panic rose up in my throat. I couldn't believe it! At the same time, it came as no surprise. It had been turned off a lot lately. But this was ridiculous. *Where was he?!* I tried his mobile again.

"The mobile number you are calling is switched off." It was infuriating and so distressing!

He returned home at three in the morning.

I was beside myself with worry. My head had not stopped pounding. I was still really sick. I felt completely invisible. I felt confused and anxious. I felt worthless.

Chapter 2: Turmoil

Walking on Eggshells

December 2009

My 40th birthday was getting closer. I think most people plan a party for their 40th or some 'big surprise'. I was really looking forward to mine. I had always said that I didn't want a party. When we'd talked about my birthday, I had said I would like to go somewhere romantic, perhaps abroad; just the two of us for a couple of days. We had only been abroad once. That was before we had the children.

The day finally arrived. We were all gathered together in the lounge. I sat on the sofa and felt a mixture of excitement and nervousness. The children huddled around me excitedly. I didn't know what to expect and I didn't know what to feel, especially after his odd behaviour over the last few weeks.

He handed me an envelope.

I took it and opened it looking into the eyes of three smiling faces. As the plane tickets fell into my lap, I felt my heart sink with disappointment. There were five! Five tickets to Amsterdam during Christmas and New Year, the busiest time of the year! I was stunned and totally confused. It was the exact opposite of what I had wanted: travelling with three children, through the cold, snow and wet. The five of us! Very unromantic! It was not at all what I had been hoping for – just more unwanted stress!

In that very moment I realised. It hit me. It was suddenly obvious that my husband didn't want to go away with just me on my own.

It took all my willpower not to react to my feelings but to force a smile and to appear excited. As soon as the children realised we were all going on holiday, they started jumping all over the place with yelps of excitement. How could I have shown my true feelings of utter disappointment? I just sat there. I didn't share their excitement. All I could think was, 'Why didn't he want to go away with me? What have I done? What is wrong with me? What is it? I don't understand!'

What I did understand was that there was something very wrong with our marriage. It was all so bewildering, so confusing and so hurtful. He had known that I wanted a romantic holiday. Instead, he had booked 'something' – 'anything', just as long as it was a 'holiday'. Not for two – not just me and him, but for all of us.

At that time, I still had no idea that he was having an affair. He wouldn't talk about what was going on. I tried to ask many times what was wrong, but he kept saying that he was tired and busy at work. His standard answer was always, "I don't know," followed by a sigh. Then he would mutter "I'm sorry," as he would turn his head away to look at the television. It was heartbreaking.

Trying to compose myself I stared intently at the tickets. All I could see was the word Amsterdam! I looked up at him and he was smiling sheepishly. I was confused. I was hurt, tremendously hurt. It was going to be the children's first time on an aeroplane. They were ecstatic! How could I possibly destroy that? I looked at them and I knew that I had to go on this holiday. I knew that I had to try to enjoy it, for their sake.

That is regret number two, right there. First, that God had warned me with the word 'infidelity' and I had chosen not to listen.

Now, secondly, I faced a similar dilemma. If *only* I had challenged him about the trip! I have looked back at that moment many times. I was too scared. I was really scared: scared of everything, scared of losing him, scared of hearing the truth maybe? Whatever the reason, I do regret saying nothing.

A couple of weeks later I went to church. My emotions were in turmoil. I was a wreck. How I had kept myself together over the last few months, I will never know. But on this day, the Sunday before Christmas Day, I was at breaking point. My whole being was in turmoil. I was under so much stress and pressure from my husband's behaviour, unanswered questions and lack of care.

For months I had carried this huge weight. It was so completely overwhelming. I had been walking around on 'eggshells' in the house, not knowing what to say to him. His attitude was so crushing. He had become more and more aloof and distant, apathetic almost: no conversation, no eye contact, nothing. I felt as if he didn't want to be in the same room as me. The atmosphere was tense, awkward and deafeningly silent.

I was at my wits' end. Back in November, he had given me a list of dates that he was planning to be out in the evenings. He had been absent a great deal since September already. He was never home for dinner any more. Most evenings he was late and his dinner was cold. He seemed completely uninterested in conversation, not just with me, but with the children as well. Family life as we knew it seemed to be slowing to a halt. Weekends didn't include family activities or outings any longer. We seemed to stop visiting family and friends too. He was hardly ever at home. In the evenings, he returned home so late that he didn't see the children before they went to bed. The days, the nights, everything was becoming unbearable.

The feeling of dread seemed to creep up on me day after day. The atmosphere in the house was intolerable. We kept everything pleasant in front of the children. When he was in the house, he focused all his attention on the children and hardly said a word to me. It felt as if he was using them as a means of avoiding talking to me.

For weeks, I hadn't slept through the night. I found it impossible to sleep when he was out so late, not knowing when he would be home. I was frantic with worry. It was a vicious circle: lack of sleep night after night, piled on with mountains of anxiety and stress. It was horrendous.

Added to this was the difficulty of his limited conversation and distant manner.

When he refused to talk to me, he almost made me feel guilty for asking him what was wrong. It seemed to be my fault. Looking back, it was a type of emotional and mental torture. I was desperately unhappy, and trying my very best to act as though nothing was wrong.

This particular Sunday I found the church service too difficult. It took all my strength to act normally. I felt as if everything was too much. I had reached my limit. At the end of the service I asked my best friend and the church leader to pray with me.

We sat at the back of the hall and I shared a few things that had been going on over the past few months.

The first question I was asked was: "Is he having an affair?" followed quickly by, "It sounds like a mid-life crisis!"

I knew that she didn't believe that he could be having an affair simply by the way she had said it. He was so respected and loved by everyone.

I broke down. I remember it so well. It was humiliating. I could not stop crying and sobbing. I was torn apart. I was a complete wreck and I had reached the point when I couldn't take any more – I just had to tell someone. I had been carrying this 'secret' for so long. I had walked around with a mask on, pretending all was OK. It was a place of denial and struggling for survival all at the same time.

I couldn't do it any more. I didn't know what to do and the weight was far too heavy. The unanswered questions in my mind were destroying me. How could I suspect my husband of having an affair? What kind of wife was I? What had I done? How could I make it better? What was wrong with him? All those late nights with his mobile turned off – where had he been and who was he with? What was he doing? Doesn't he understand how hurt I am, what pain I am in? Does he love me? The questions burned.

It was too much to bear. Everything in my heart tumbled out. Once I started confiding I couldn't stop. I told them everything.

Tears rolled down my face. I was shaking uncontrollably, sobbing, shoulders hunched over in agony. I was empty. I was confused. But somehow, throughout it all, I honestly believed in my husband.

My two friends put their arms around me and prayed for me. They advised me to ask my husband three things:

First, whether or not we could meet with my Pastor together to discuss our marriage. Secondly, if not, whether my husband would allow me to speak to my Pastor about what I was feeling. Thirdly, whether or not he would be prepared to go to marriage counselling with me.

I went home. I bravely asked him all three questions. The first he refused. The second he agreed to; he even said, "If you think that might help you, then it's OK if you want to speak to the Pastor." The third, he refused and said he didn't need to go to marriage counselling.

I met with my Pastor and his wife a few days later. It was very kind of them to see me with all the busyness of Christmas.

I sat and explained everything to them. My Pastor said, "It sounds as if he is either going through a mid-life crisis or having an affair."

I remember so clearly what my Pastor said next. "The man I know," he said, "would never lie." He said it with a passionate conviction and it was so true. I nodded my head in agreement and so did his wife.

It just goes to show that as human beings we really want to believe the best in people.

We continued to speak and decided that however hard it was right now, I had to try my best to make Christmas a good time for the sake of the children.

I'm really thankful for that advice. Christmas was daunting. It was meant to be a wonderful family time, and the trip to Amsterdam was only a few days after that. I had to do my best to keep everything as normal as possible for the children.

And I did.

Chapter 3: Doing My Best

All for the Children

> *Psalm 73:26*
> *My flesh and my heart may fail, but God is the strength of my heart and my portion for ever.*

Christmas 2009

Christmas was really hard. It was a lie really. It was a complete pretence. Sad as it is, that is the truth.

Just a few days before Christmas I told my husband what my Pastor had said. I asked him what was wrong and again he replied that he didn't know. I suggested that perhaps it would be best not to talk about it again until we came back from holiday. We agreed and the tension was slightly relieved.

Not knowing what was wrong was the hardest part. I really thought that he was going through a 'mid-life crisis' and I convinced myself that if I tried to be the best wife I could be, then he would 'snap out of it' and everything would be back to the way it was before this all started.

We did our best to keep things as normal as possible, hanging stockings on bedroom doors and giving each other presents on Christmas morning. We even took photos as though we were the happiest family in town; except we weren't. I don't think the children noticed anything out of place. They seemed to enjoy the day.

We went to my parents' house for Christmas dinner. He was very quiet. After dessert, it was normally he who would sit by the tree and would hand out the presents to the family. But not this year. He did not move. Quickly, I smiled and brushed it off and took up the role myself, trying hard to make it fun. It was exhausting. It felt wrong. I felt as if I was lying to everyone; hiding this huge secret. No-one knew what was going on.

A few days later we packed our bags and drove to the airport. We boarded the plane with three very excited children and embarked on my 'birthday treat' to Amsterdam. It was as if I was acting: playing the part of the perfect Mummy, wanting my children to be happy and not suspecting that anything was wrong. But inside, I was dying. I was so very miserable. I hadn't wanted to go. I didn't want to be there.

Amsterdam was busy, snowing and bitterly cold. I was increasingly conscious of just how glamorous the women looked. They wore exquisite, long flowing, fur-lined coats, with collars and cuffs, accompanied by matching hats and expensive leather boots. I was wearing my short blue, fleece-lined jacket and moss-green walking boots. I felt out of place and extremely unattractive. We were on a small budget and before long we found ourselves traipsing up and down the streets, desperately searching for somewhere cheap to eat.

During our trip we tried to absorb as many of the usual tourist hot spots as possible. We visited a few art galleries, went on a sightseeing barge down the canal, walked around the lakes and browsed in all the shops. But all I noticed was the huge invisible wall between us. He walked up front, leaving me trailing behind, as was now 'normal'. I hated it. I look back and can't believe I agreed to go! But at the time I felt as if I had no choice as the children were my top priority.

My heart was breaking. I felt like a robot. We had gone away together, yet it seemed as if I was with a complete stranger. Between us there was no depth of conversation. We probably looked like the 'perfect family' to outsiders, yet it was far from the truth. We were pretending.

I struggle to imagine what was going through his mind. Who knows? But I knew what was going through mine. I felt completely alone, yet surrounded by people in a very busy place. I felt like crying, yet I had to stay composed at all times 'for the sake of the children'. I felt trapped, isolated, scared: scared of the unknown, scared of what was going on behind his silent facade. He seemed to be always looking at his phone. I would ask who texted him and he would reply that it was one of his friends from work. He was continually writing texts.

It was so noticeable that he didn't love me. He didn't hold my hand when we walked down the street. He walked up ahead instead. He didn't look at me. There is a recognisable 'look' between two people in love. That look that seems to go beyond the eyes to the soul? He didn't look at me like that any more.

I felt weak: not physically, but emotionally. I was tired. As a Christian, I've always depended on God, and as I prayed during those difficult moments I thanked Him for giving me strength as He had promised in Isaiah 40:31: *"But those who hope in the Lord will renew their strength."* God was my Strength. I put my trust and my hope in Him.

The holiday in Amsterdam is not one of my greatest memories! Certainly I would never like to go there again.

I look back and I ask myself now, why did I agree to go? *Why did I?* The only answer I can give is that hindsight makes the pitfalls easier to see. It certainly is a different story when you are 'in' it. I did what I thought was best at the time for the sake of the children. Maybe in some crazy part of my thinking I thought the holiday would help.

I know that I approached Christmas and the holiday to Amsterdam with integrity. I did my very best. Today, I am a great deal stronger. I am my own person. I hope that I am strong enough to confront issues when they arise. And strength was exactly what I needed for the days ahead.

February 2010

> *Psalm 91:1*
> *He who <u>dwells</u> in the shelter of the Most High, will <u>rest</u> in the shadow*
> *of the Almighty.*

One day I was praying and I felt God say to me: "Rest in Me."

How could I rest? My life was a mess. My marriage was a mess. My husband made me feel as if I was invisible. I was worried and anxious every minute of the day. How I wanted to rest! I desperately needed to rest.

But how could I? Lying down for an hour would not have been of any use; it wasn't physical rest I needed, but mental and emotional rest. My mind was working overtime. My emotions were all over the place.

I had not spoken to another person about the anxiety I was feeling since Christmas. That was the hardest part: acting as if everything was fine, smiling, putting on a brave face wherever I went.

Hiding the truth from my family and friends was really tough. Many, many times I just wanted to scream, "Help me! My marriage is in a mess and I don't know what to do! I'm in so much pain!"

Looking back, I don't know why I didn't tell my family. I so desperately wanted to believe in my husband. Even following the conversation with my Pastor and his wife, I still could not entertain the thought that he might be having an affair. The signs were all there – but I refused to see them. I loved him. I simply couldn't bring myself to speak to anyone about it, not even my Mum. I just couldn't; I was so scared.

The scripture said: *"He who dwells …"* I wanted to be the "He". I wanted to dwell with God. If I dwelt with God – prayed with Him, spent time with Him, leaned on Him and relied on Him – then God promised to give me "rest".

The words in that scripture really spoke to me that particular day in February. When I was praying, a picture came into my mind. It played out vividly, almost like a scene from a movie. I'll describe it the best way that I can:

Imagine going out for a walk on a hot sunny day. You have been walking for a long time. There, in the distance, you see an enormous sprawling tree. You walk up to it, tired and thirsty. You slump down, leaning your back against the massive tree trunk under the big wide branches. You sigh. Shade, cooling shade, from the tree covers you. What a perfect place to stop and rest!

To me that is what God is like. He provides shelter to the weary, He provides rest "in the shadow of the Almighty". He Himself is the Almighty. He is like the tree: a place of refuge, a place of rest and shelter from the heat of our struggles.

If you are in a place of struggle, know that the Bible says that God is with you. God loves you!

I can imagine that big old sprawling tree. It is safe. It is uncomplicated, uncluttered and spacious.

Sometimes God shows us such simple things. I knew when I saw that picture and read that Psalm that I had been feeling as if I was caught up in a tornado. It was claustrophobic and unending. My emotions were all over the place. I was constantly on the verge of tears.

The weeks that followed were very difficult.

> *Psalm 73:23-28*
> *Yet I am always with you; you hold me by my right hand. You guide me with your counsel, and afterwards you will take me into glory. Whom have I in heaven but you? Earth has nothing I desire besides you. My flesh and my heart may fail, but God is the strength of my heart and my portion for ever...But as for me, it is good to be near God. I have made the Sovereign Lord my refuge; I will tell of all your deeds.*

My Mum came to my workplace. She was very upset. Thanks to my boss, we found a quiet empty office to sit in. I asked her what was wrong. She said that she had just come from the hospital. She had been diagnosed with breast cancer.

I couldn't believe it! Breast cancer! My Mum?

We both sat there crying. As I looked at her, all I could think was Mum needs me. I needed to stay strong. Mum knew nothing about my situation. I still hadn't told my family. I hadn't wanted to worry them. Maybe I was in denial, thinking it would all 'get better'.

As I sat there looking at my Mum, I felt so sad. I couldn't quite take in what she had said. I was in shock. It was hard to process that Mum had breast cancer and at the same time, I didn't want to worry her. She had enough to cope with.

Breast cancer! The words alone brought fear to my heart. As she spoke the words in a soft whisper, they sounded deafening to my ears.

The first thing I said was "Mum, let's pray." I believe God is our healer. He is our Rock, our Saviour, our Redeemer.

The days that followed were even harder.

My husband had been out twenty-nine times between October 2009 and January 2010. I know that because I had kept a diary. When I realised the number I found it even more disheartening and disappointing.

Where had he been going? He had said that he had been out to 'work-do's; out with friends from work; to the cinema in London, etc.. He came home later and later. Mostly, around 3am. He always was full of excuses such as 'missed the bus'; 'worked late', etc.

During this time he refused point blank to speak to me about what was going on. He had this attitude that it was OK and it made me feel very guilty for asking him or challenging him on his behaviour.

One evening, after the children had gone to bed, we were in the lounge and I was really struggling.

"I really need a hug," I said. He was sitting on the couch. He turned his head and looked at me. He shrugged his shoulders, looked back to the television and said: "Sorry."

I froze. I was taken aback. All I could do was stare at him in disbelief. He still had his head turned away from me, towards the television. I felt utterly humiliated.

There have been a few incidents about which I can't write here, but I've shared this one because it was so painful. There was I, his wife, looking at him asking for a hug and there was my husband saying: 'Sorry' – as if I were a piece of dirt on his shoe – nothing – absolutely nothing to him.

I don't think I have the right words to type about how he made me feel. I felt so crushed, belittled, unloved, and pathetic.

I went upstairs, sat on our bed and sobbed. He didn't once appear. He stayed downstairs.

After about an hour I went down. Immediately, he leaned forward from the sofa, stood up and announced that he was going out. *Going out?* I couldn't believe what I was hearing! *Going out?* Now? *Where to?*

"To play pool with ... from work," he said coldly.

I sank into the chair opposite his in total shock. *Was I completely invisible?*

What was going on? What was wrong with me? What had I done? Why did he treat me so badly? I didn't understand it. He was so thoughtless, detached and uncaring.

Where had my husband gone? Who was he? This was not him? He was so cruel.

He grabbed his coat, swept up his car keys and left. He left me just sitting there.

He had had many opportunities to tell me the truth.

I had asked him whether he was having an affair a couple of times. It took a great deal of courage to even utter the question.

Both times he denied it vehemently. This left me feeling guilty that I had doubted him and I was totally confused.

One evening in February we were both sitting in the lounge when again I asked him what was wrong. I kept asking him, wanting him to explain to me what he was thinking and feeling.

Suddenly, without warning, he leapt from the sofa and stood close to the television. It startled me. He was shifting from one foot to the other, clutching his hair. Then, he exploded in frustration:

"I don't love you any more! You have changed! You are old! I can't do anything I want to!"

I didn't understand what he was talking about.

"What are you going to do?" I asked him.

He said that he didn't know and that he didn't know whether he would stay or move out.

What?

Move out?

What on earth was he talking about? I asked him questions and all he could reply was: "I don't know."

It's really hard talking to someone who doesn't want to talk back, someone who doesn't want to open up or say what's on their mind. On the other hand, I was clinging to the edge of my seat, desperate for him to tell me what was going on. But he simply stood there staring at the carpet, shaking his head, clutching his hair and refusing to explain what he had meant.

I had planned to go with my eldest daughter a few days later to see my good friend in Norwich and stay with her for a few days. Minutes after we arrived, I was standing in her kitchen leaning on the tiled worktop. She casually asked me how I was and I started crying. I didn't mean to. Maybe it was the way she looked at me or the fact that I trusted her and I was in a safe place. In that moment I had come to the end. I couldn't stand there and lie for another moment. I was finished. I was filled with so much pain, turmoil and confusion that I couldn't stand there and pretend that everything was OK. I melted. I began to share a little bit of what was going on.

She asked if he was having an affair, and I replied that he had said he wasn't. So she also put it down to a mid-life crisis. It didn't sound like the man she knew.

After much discussion, she suggested I should phone a solicitor for some advice in case he decided to move out. A few days later, while still at my friend's house, although it took a great deal of courage, I picked up the phone to make an appointment with a solicitor. I felt so overwhelmed by guilt. I didn't know what to do. All I could think about was what my husband would say. What if things got better? Phoning a solicitor seemed so very serious. Was my situation really that serious?

The next day I phoned and cancelled the appointment. I was so afraid. I was afraid of his reaction, I was afraid of everything!

My eldest daughter and I arrived home on Tuesday 16th February. We walked into the lounge. He was there. He didn't even ask me how the trip was or how my friend was. He simply ignored me. A little while later, I tried once again to talk to him. Deliberately, softly and directly, I asked him whether he was having an affair.

He turned from the screen, glared at me, dropped the remote controllers down in his lap and spat out the words furiously: "No! Don't you trust me?"

Then quite simply he announced, "I think it would be best for us if I move out."

What on earth was he talking about? ...Best for 'us'? Says who? It was certainly not best for me or the children!

I hung my head and burst into tears. I rushed to my feet, picked up my keys and ran down the stairs and out of the front door.

I drove to my Pastor's house and knocked on the door. I went into their kitchen and sobbed and sobbed. I was so upset. I didn't know what was going on and neither did they. All my Pastor and his wife could do was comfort me and pray with me.

The following day was Wednesday. My husband was due to go on holiday by himself abroad to see his brother for a week. He had planned it a while earlier but he hadn't given me any flight details. Just before he was due to leave I asked him for a copy of his itinerary. He said he didn't have one and got very agitated with me.

I said that I needed to know what time his plane was leaving. Because I was insistent, he then let slip that he actually would not be seeing his brother until Sunday. At that point alarm bells started ringing – today was only Wednesday! My thoughts were racing – Sunday? So what was he doing in the meantime?

He grabbed a piece of paper and scribbled down the time of departure and arrival back to London. He said that his plane was leaving the next morning and he would be spending the night in the airport. He would be leaving the house shortly.

He went out to the shops. I couldn't breathe. I was panicking. I went upstairs. I saw his bag on the floor in the bedroom. I opened one zip. There was a printed copy of his planned itinerary. He had lied! I couldn't really read it because my hands were shaking uncontrollably. I was so much in a panic worrying that he would be back any second and see me going through his bag.

I took a deep breath, closed the door and opened the main zip of the bag. Inside were his clothes and under them were three or four DVD shaped presents. All were wrapped in girly flowery paper. I remember being completely beside myself with panic.

All I kept thinking was, *'Where is he going? Who are the presents for? Yes, it is his brother's birthday – but they are not presents gift-wrapped for a man! Who are they for? He's having an affair! Oh my goodness!'* I quickly zipped up the bag and went downstairs. Within seconds, he came home. I was worried sick!

What do I say? Do I ask him? I was very fearful of his reaction, and what if I had got it wrong?

He said a brief goodbye to the children and left the house. I knew. I knew. I knew that he was having an affair. I knew it! But I still wanted to believe him so desperately.

Friday 19th February 2010

On Friday evening I had asked my Dad to come over to my house. I wanted to tell him that my husband was thinking of leaving. I didn't know what to do. I wanted to tell my Mum but she had just been diagnosed with cancer. I didn't know whether or not the timing was right.

I told my Dad briefly what I knew, which was nothing much. My husband had said he wasn't having an affair, so I didn't know what else to say except that we might be separating.

Mum was due to have her first operation in a couple of weeks. We decided that it was best to wait until my husband came back and had made a decision. We didn't want to worry her, not at this time. It seemed unfair to place this massive burden onto her shoulders as well. She was going through a difficult time herself.

Later that evening I sat at our home computer. I opened the inbox. The first thing I noticed was that a huge chunk of time and dates were missing. I remembered that a few days before the trip to my friends' there had been an incident in the study. He had been in there on the computer for ages. I needed to send a quick email. He wasn't very happy about it. When I sat in the chair he seemed nervous and flustered loitering behind me, telling me not to be long. I had my own user account so I didn't even look at his emails or what he was doing. It didn't occur to me.

Now I started to open each email from September 2009. I quickly discovered that there were a few emails with the subject box saying "football" or something similar. When I opened them, they were composed of only a short sentence but I noticed that I could move the scroll bar down the page even though there were only a few words at the top. What I discovered were 'secret' emails from a woman. I only found a few, but it was enough to confirm that he was indeed having an affair.

My heart inside my chest was pounding in horror. I couldn't believe it! The emails were not sordid or anything like that, but it was clear that they were more than friends.

Next I discovered emails confirming tickets purchased by my husband in November and December. They were for two people.

I ran upstairs to get my diary. Each event corresponded with the nights he was 'out with work'.

Then I went through our bank statements. I noticed that he had withdrawn over £500 in November in total, and again in December using his cashpoint card. He had also made a purchase in a ladies' clothing shop for £80. Each withdrawal corresponded to the dates he was 'out with work'.

There are no words to describe how I felt. I was absolutely and utterly in shock. I was in so much pain that I can't describe it.

I went to bed that Friday evening and I prayed. I prayed to God a very, very, very desperate prayer. It was something like this: "God, please, please, please, I need to know the truth, I need to find SOMETHING. I need proof. Please God, *please* God, *please God*, help me, *please!*"

Chapter 4: The Day My World Fell Apart

The Truth is Revealed

> *Psalm 116:3-4*
> *The cords of death entangled me, the anguish of the grave came upon me; I was overcome by trouble and sorrow. Then I called on the name of the Lord: "O Lord, save me!"*

Saturday 20th February 2010

The next day I woke up very early: 5.30am.

As soon as I opened my eyes, I knew. I *knew* that I had to open the top drawer of our computer desk in the study. I had no idea why, but I felt it in my whole being. There was a sense of urgency.

I jumped out of bed, put on my dressing gown and went downstairs. I walked into the study and perched on the edge of the chair.

I opened the top drawer of the desk. This was my husband's drawer. It wasn't locked, but was accessible to everyone. Everyone knew though, that it was his drawer for his work papers. I had opened it millions of times, looking for a pen or scrap of paper.

As I opened it, I put my hand inside the drawer and moved the contents slightly. A carefully folded piece of paper fell out of a tiny padded envelope.

I opened it. It was an A4 sheet of paper. It was not his writing. I started reading the first line and my heart started thumping inside my chest, my eyes wide in horror. It was a love letter, a poem really, but a love letter nonetheless.

I

could

not

believe

it.

I recoiled in shock, feeling sick. Still reading the letter I leapt from the chair and stepped into the kitchen. My eyes were growing wider with every awful word. I found I was gripping the paper tightly, and it felt as though the walls of the kitchen were closing in around me, crushing every last ounce of life from my body. Finding it difficult to breathe, I was struggling to stay on my feet, to stand, to cope with the intense weight of what I was reading.

Right at the bottom of the page I noticed it: two letters. They were the same initials as the lady's name, the one I had asked him about back in November after I had looked at his phone! It couldn't be a coincidence. To make matters worse, it was so obvious she was talking about him. It confirmed *everything* that had happened over the last six months. My husband, *MY husband,* was having an affair! Every word, every line that I read and re-read in disbelief was like a slap to my face. I could not believe it! Tears filled my eyes and started tumbling down my cheeks. As I read it to the end, the waves of realisation – that he had slept with somebody else, that he had lied to my face, and that the writer was deeply in love with my husband – swept over me, causing my knees to buckle.

I collapsed, crumpling in a heap, face-down on the kitchen floor.

That was the day, the very moment, my world fell apart.

I was lying on the freezing wooden floor, sobbing and sobbing and sobbing. I was in so much pain that I was unable to stand up. The torment of finding out he was having an affair was so utterly awful. In all my years, I have never ever experienced such agony. I was shaking uncontrollably. Time seemed to stand still.

I couldn't believe it! Not him! Not my husband! I believed him! I BELIEVED HIM! HOW COULD HE? No! No! NO!

I was there for over an hour but it seemed like forever. My legs had turned to jelly. I slowly picked myself off the floor, went into the lounge and snatched up the phone. I walked back into the kitchen and stared at it in my hand. I didn't know what to do. My mind was racing. I couldn't think straight.

I knelt to the floor. I couldn't phone my Mum. Only two weeks before, she had only been diagnosed with breast cancer. She didn't need this. I was in such a mess. I knelt there, still crying. I dialled the number of my mother-in-law.

When she answered the phone, I could hardly speak, let alone speak coherently.

It all gushed out at once, "He is having an affair! I can't believe it! *I can't believe it!* I've found this letter in his drawer. How could he? HOW COULD HE?" I was screaming and crying at the same time down the phone. I still couldn't take it all in. It was all too much to bear. It didn't seem real.

My mother-in-law was very calm, and her voice went very quiet. She kept saying, "Toni, I'm going to get on the bus and come over right now. OK? Right now! Just stay there."

I don't know how many times she said it. Eventually, I replied, "OK." I was barely able to breathe.

As soon as I put the phone down, I ran to get my mobile and started searching for my husband's number. Frantically I jabbed the buttons. "This person's phone is switched off. Please try later ..." I was beside myself! I was very angry, yet at the same time so scared!

I paced up and down the kitchen – up and down, up and down. I didn't know what to do. I couldn't believe it! How could he have his phone switched off? Where was he? What was he doing?

My life was falling apart and his phone was switched off!

I kept saying aloud, "How could he? How could he?! I can't believe it. I … can't … believe … it!" Tears continued to roll down my face while gut-wrenching sobs burst out of my mouth intermittently.

The pain was so agonising: the realisation that my husband had been lying to me was simply too much to take in. I was in shock. I felt like a complete idiot. I couldn't understand how or why he would do that? All those lies. He had lied and lied and lied and lied and lied! And I had BELIEVED him!

I tried his phone again and left him a message to ring me urgently.

The wait was horrendous. It seemed to take forever.

Then, finally, he texted me: "You can call me now."

I was furious. As I picked up the phone and rang his number my hands were shaking, and my teeth were still chattering with shock. I leaned heavily against one of the kitchen chairs, still struggling to stand.

When he answered, I said in the calmest voice I could muster, "I am going to ask you for the last time, and I want the truth: are you having an affair?"

"No," he said!

"Well," I replied, in as constrained a way as I could manage, "Let me read you something then …" I tried desperately to keep myself from exploding, while being absolutely frantic inside.

I started reading the first line of the love poem.

"OK! OK!" he said.

"SO ARE YOU HAVING AN AFFAIR?" I screamed down the phone.

"Well, I think you know the answer," he said in a very quiet voice.

Furiously I shouted: "Well, I want *you* to tell me the truth!"

"Yes," he replied even more quietly.

I lost my temper and screamed, "HOW COULD YOU?"

I have only ever raised my voice like that twice. This was the first time.

I was crying and sobbing. "BUT I TRUSTED YOU! I BELIEVED YOU! HOW COULD YOU? DO YOU KNOW WHAT YOU HAVE DONE? YOU HAVE DESTROYED OUR MARRIAGE! YOU HAVE DESTROYED ME… US! HOW COULD YOU LIE TO ME?"

Then, I needed answers. I needed the truth. "Who is she?"

"Someone from work," he replied.

"How long has it been going on?" I demanded.

"Since September," he said, his voice getting quieter.

"September!" I screamed. I couldn't believe it. September! I had asked him at Christmas if he was having an affair, and *he* had denied it and *he* had made *me* feel incredibly guilty! September!

All these thoughts were pounding around my head at full speed. I could hardly think straight. I couldn't take in what he was telling me. It was too much.

He had lied. He had made me feel as if it was my fault; as if everything was my fault; as if I was the one with the problem! For weeks I had dreaded coming in through the front door into the unknown.

I had even poured my heart out to my Pastor and his wife. He had given me permission to meet with them to talk about what might be wrong! I felt totally humiliated! And the holiday! He made me go on that holiday! He had treated me like rubbish, yet all this time he had been with another woman! Secretly meeting her at all hours; secretly emailing her; secretly taking her to concerts and events, and leaving me at home with the children, worried sick.

I stood there, gripping the evidence in my hand, leaning my full weight on the chair.

"How many times have you slept with her?" I demanded.

"I'm not going to answer that; it will only cause you more pain." His reply was barely audible.

I have always remembered that. I know it sounds silly, but I remember being so shocked with that answer – MORE PAIN? How was that ever possible?

I was clinging to the back of the chair to stop myself from falling to the floor and insisted that he got on the first plane home to the UK – "NOW! RIGHT NOW!"

I was so distraught that I can't even remember if he said sorry at that point.

He said he would do his best to get home as soon as he could, although I doubted him; there seemed to be a lack of urgency in his voice.

Then he pleaded softly, "Please don't put my stuff outside, please …"

I put the phone down.

I was in shock. For some time I stood there, doubled over the chair, crying, my legs struggling to hold me up.

After a while, I picked up the phone and rang my Pastor and his wife and asked them to come and take my girls to their house for the day. I explained what had happened as best as I could. They said that they would come.

After speaking to them, I walked upstairs with a roll of black bags and put them on my bed. I wanted everything OUT! I wanted everything of his gone from our bedroom! I wanted his 'stuff' as far away from me as possible. Just looking at it suddenly repulsed me. My stomach was in knots. I looked around our room and all I could see were his things everywhere.

I picked up my towel and walked quietly into the bathroom and locked the door. I had a shower, got dressed and tried to sort myself out.

Then, as I stood in front of the open wardrobe, I unrolled one bag and tore it from the roll. I was desperately struggling to hold back the tears. I clenched my teeth together and opened the bag. I felt so emotional. Anger rose up within me as I looked at his clothes. Without hesitation, I reached up and began yanking his clothes from the hangers and stuffing them into the black bag.

At around 10am my youngest daughter came into the bedroom. "Mummy, what are you doing?" she asked.

"Oh, just sorting out some of Daddy's clothes to take to the charity," I said.

She looked rather worried. I had filled four or five black bags by now.

"OK," she said.

It was the way she kept looking from the bags to me that melted my heart. She looked so uneasy. I immediately stopped filling the bag, put it down and closed the wardrobe door. I smiled at her and said in a very gentle voice, "The pastor and his wife are coming to collect you and your sister in a few minutes. They are taking you to their house to play with their children today. Isn't that nice? They will be here in a minute. Do you want to get ready?"

"OK," she said. She didn't seem terribly sure what was going on but I didn't want to worry her further. I was trying to be as normal as possible.

It was right then that I realised how great God was.

My children hadn't heard me shouting, screaming, crying or sobbing down the phone to their Dad. They hadn't witnessed me lying on the floor in tears either. They had slept through everything.

How amazing! I sat on my bed among the bags. God is so wonderful. I knew that God protected my children.

I had been *really* screaming down the phone. I'm surprised my neighbours hadn't banged on the front door. Maybe God had protected them from hearing too!

I was probably on the telephone for about 45 minutes. That's a long time to be screaming? I am so very grateful to God for protecting them that morning. They had absolutely no idea of what had happened.

My Pastor's wife collected the children. I tried my best to smile, thanking her over and over again for coming. As we gathered coats and shoes, I tried to make it sound like a morning of fun for the children. I kissed them as they were leaving. They looked a little quizzically at me, but they seemed to go without any fuss.

Then, just as they were leaving, there was another knock at the door. It was my mother-in-law. As soon as she walked in, I started crying and sobbing all over again. She sat with me until lunchtime, listening to my sobbing, crying and shouting. I asked her to ring her three sons and tell them what my husband had done. I was adamant that I wanted them to hear the truth, not some fabrication from him.

I look back now and I don't know what good, if any, that did, but the realisation that he had lied repeatedly to me made me think, 'What has he been saying to them?' They deserved to know the truth.

By early afternoon I had calmed down enough to stop crying. My mother-in-law and I went together to tell my parents and my Nan. They were completely shocked as they struggled to take it all in.

I was worried about my Mum too. As I sat there on the sofa, she hugged me. I felt so terrible, so terrible for everything, and to make matters worse, only the evening before, I had chosen to tell Mum nothing.

It was a big mistake. It hurt my Mum deeply when she found out that Dad had known first and we had decided not to tell her straightaway.

We thought we were making the right decision. We had no idea that in a few hours I would be in a crumpled heap on my kitchen floor holding a love letter in my hand.

We had no idea that my world would fall apart. Nevertheless, I looked into my Mum's eyes and I saw the pain. No matter how much we wanted to protect her, I had let her down. It was not the right decision. She felt hurt and left out.

Not only that, but she was also incredibly disappointed that I had kept silent for the last six months and had not confided in her. They were all disappointed.

I have made mistakes and this was one of them. Sometimes we have to trust those we love enough to let them into our hearts – even if it means they may worry.

"Mum, I'm so sorry. I just didn't want to worry you. I just wanted you to get better; to get through the operation. I never meant to hurt you. I thought I could deal with it all on my own. How wrong I was. I love you."

After a few more cups of tea, my mother-in-law and I went to collect the children. I was so grateful to my Pastor and his wife for looking after them, for keeping them safe and for giving me time to speak to my family.

When they got into the car, I could tell that they knew something was wrong. My Pastor's wife had said to me that she had told them, "Mummy has some things to deal with and will explain it to you when she is ready." They looked at me with those big eyes full of questions. But they jumped into the car and we drove my mother-in-law's home.

I didn't say anything to the children about what had happened. I didn't know what to say and I didn't want to worry them either. I wanted everything to be 'normal' for the children until my husband returned.

Chapter 5: 7 Days of Agony

Waiting

Sunday 21st February 2010

The next day was Sunday. I had hardly slept. I woke very early again and went to sit at the computer. At 8.38am I sent an email to my husband's mistress. I had her email address from the 'secret' emails that I had found on Friday evening.

I had to write to her. I had to tell her exactly what she had done to me.

I wrote and re-wrote that email many times before I sent it.

I wanted her to know that she and my husband were equally to blame. I was not so naïve that I blamed her entirely.

She knew he was married with three children. So did he.

They both knew the consequences of their actions the moment they stepped over the line into a path of lies, deceit, and lust.

A marriage should be respected. No woman should touch a married man. I believe a woman who does so is a woman who is devoid of integrity.

I also believe a married man who allows himself to get into an adulterous relationship, loses not only his integrity, but also his reputation. Trust is eliminated from all relationships at every level.

I wanted the email to state only the truth. I did not say anything rude nor did I slander her in any way. I wanted to act in an honourable way; I didn't want anything in that email to be offensive.

This is the email I sent her:

> Yesterday morning I found a love letter from you in my husband's desk drawer. When I asked him about it, he said that you and he had been having an affair for months.
>
> By having an affair with my husband, you and he have completely and utterly destroyed our marriage, our family and, soon, our children. You may or may not be married or have children, but I have a husband and I have three children; we have been married for 17 years. You are both responsible. You both know right from wrong and you both know what self-control is, yet you both failed to exercise it.
>
> Do not be fooled by him saying that 'we drifted apart, etc.' That is a complete lie.
>
> What you may not realise, yet he realises fully, is just how much the children love their Daddy. They completely adore

him; their faces light up when he walks into the room. This will completely destroy their faith in him. This will absolutely, and without a doubt, totally crush them.

He has not just lied to me, but to our children, our family, our friends, and his friends. The pain that both of you have caused has already started to impact our extended family. When he returns from abroad shortly, he will have to look his three children in the eye and tell them the truth of both of your actions. It will be absolutely heartbreaking.

As I pressed the send button my hands were shaking, my heart was pounding and I couldn't stop crying.

I hoped she would receive it, but at the same time I dreaded her replying to it. I hoped she wouldn't. But a couple of days later she did reply.

The morning I sent that email I was determined to act as normally as possible. I turned off the computer and got ready for church.

We stood at the back that morning and I just cried during worship. I stood next to one of my best friends. The children kept asking me why I was crying. I kept saying I was OK and tried my best to smile and hug them. They kept looking at me with worried faces.

Part of the service was my Pastor's son's baptism. We were invited to stay on afterwards for the celebration meal. It was a blur. I couldn't eat. I tried to look composed but it was very difficult. I have come to the conclusion that I'm very good at 'appearing normal' when in actual fact I'm in a complete crisis; or another way to put it is: I'm rather convincing at 'wearing a mask'.

That afternoon I received a text from my husband saying that the earliest flight home was Monday evening. He would be home around 10pm. It was too long. It was devastating. It felt as though he wasn't trying hard enough. I felt unimportant. I felt as if I wasn't worth rushing home for. There was no sense of urgency! Just a simple phone call to say there was nothing else he could do that would have helped. I didn't understand why he couldn't have done something. I had no choice but to wait.

When I spoke to him again on the phone, I made it very clear that he was to come straight home from the airport! He was not to go anywhere else, or meet HER anywhere. It all sounds rather futile. I couldn't believe a word he said. I telephoned his brother and asked him to stay with him and make sure he got on the plane home. I also asked him to email me the flight details so I could see for myself whether or not he was telling the truth.

I am grateful to my brother-in-law that he did email me with the details. It put me at ease a little, and he reassured me that he would stay with him until he got on the plane.

On Sunday evening, one of my best friends came to my house. I was frantically cleaning. So we cleaned together. I had to do something. Cleaning the kitchen and the study was suddenly an absolute necessity. My poor friend!

I smile now when I think of it. She came round to sit with me and ended up being bossed about by me with commands to clean this and that. I am so grateful to her. We both cleaned until I was so tired I had to stop.

Later that evening, I went onto the computer to see if there were any replies following my email to my husband's mistress. I couldn't look. I was a nervous wreck. I was shaking. I simply couldn't look at the inbox. My friend checked but there was no reply. Phew! I couldn't have faced it even if there was a reply. I was so relieved.

Monday 22nd February 2010

The next day was Monday. My husband was due to arrive home that evening around 10pm.

I made sure that the children were tucked up in bed early. They still didn't know what was going on. At around 8.30pm I walked into the lounge and closed the door. I spent a long time praying. I walked up and down my lounge praying.

10pm came and went. A while later I got a text from my husband saying that he had missed the bus and would be home when he could. I was upset and felt very confused. Where was he?

I waited, and waited and waited. It was agonising! All I kept thinking was: "Where was he? What was he doing? Who was he with? WHERE WAS HE?" We live ten minutes' drive from the train station. Missing the bus I could forgive, but there was another bus every 15 minutes which stopped 15 minutes' walk away! There was no excuse about missing buses!

Was I not important enough for him to come home to? Obviously not! Was our marriage important to him? Obviously not! It was completely unbearable! I had been waiting since Saturday morning to see him. Now it was Monday evening, over sixty hours later *and* he was still refusing to come home! I didn't understand what was going on! Where was he?

I kept pacing up and down, up and down. I couldn't sit down, I had to keep moving. I was on tenterhooks.

I texted him around 11.30pm. "Where are you?" I demanded.

"Waiting for the bus," was his reply.

I was so angry. He was at the train station, less than ten minutes away by car. *Or was he? Was he lying? What was he doing?*

"There are such things as taxis," I texted back.

Tuesday 23rd February 2010

Finally, at 12.30am on Tuesday, I heard the familiar click of the front door.

It was two and a half hours after he was due to be home. They were the longest two hours of my life. He walked into the lounge, his head hanging down and not looking me in the eye.

Miraculously, by this time I was very calm. I am so thankful to God for that. I had prayed constantly all of that time, and by the time he walked in I was ready. I was sitting in the chair, alert and calm.

I didn't know what he was expecting to come home to but I'm sure he was not expecting that. I think he was expecting all his stuff to be sitting outside in black sacks with his wife raging at him. But that was not the case, and I was not angry. I was too worn out. I was tired yet fully awake.

When he sat down on the couch opposite me I spoke in a quiet voice. "How could you?"

He looked down at the floor. His reaction was not the reaction I had hoped for or expected.

I had pictured it very different from how it actually happened. I thought he would come through the front door, saying he was desperately sorry and begging me to forgive him. I wanted him to say that his mistress meant nothing to him; pleading with me for us to work it out … holding me.

I was not prepared for his reaction. I was totally wrong.

Instead, he sat on the couch completely silent, still not looking at me.

Rather than the scenario I had been hoping for, he said: "It's too late. I don't want to talk about it now."

I felt so crushed. *Who was this person opposite me? Was he really my husband? Was he secretly hoping that I would have given up hours earlier and gone to bed?* I don't know. I have no idea what was going through his head. But he wasn't someone I recognised. In that one sentence he had taken control and made me feel very scared and frightened.

I knew then that, whatever I could say, he had made his mind up and our marriage was over.

But I wanted to talk about it. I was not going to bed now! I sat there and calmly asked a few questions. He nodded in places, but didn't speak much. There was no feeling. There was no emotion from him.

All those lies! Sleeping with another woman! All for what? I asked him if he was leaving. He didn't know what his plans were. He just sat there, eyes toward the floor, no passion of heart, cold, apathetic.

It was then that I said to him that if he was leaving he would have to look his children in the eye and tell them the truth. I wouldn't be doing it. Neither would they hear it from someone else. He would have to do it.

At this, he got angry and agitated. He said, "They are just children! I can't tell them that! No! I won't!"

"Yes, you will," I said calmly. "You are their Dad and you owe it to them to tell them the truth."

I can't remember what else we said in those early hours, but I asked him lots of questions. I still remained calm. I still spoke in a quiet, soft voice. No anger. No raised voice.

I didn't want him sleeping on the couch. I was so worried about the children that I wanted everything to appear normal. After a while, we went to bed and said that when the children went to school the next day we would talk. It was very awkward. It was really difficult. I could hardly sleep.

How could he have done this? How could he have slept with someone else for months? How could he have lied and lied continuously? What was going to happen? I felt so exhausted. My stomach was churning with anxiety. *How* could this be happening to us?

The children were very surprised and excited to see their Daddy in the morning. They kept asking why he had come back early. He said that there were things that Mummy and Daddy needed to sort out.

It was a normal school day. I got the children ready for school and walked our youngest to the school gate. I look back now and wonder how I did that but I was their Mum and they needed me. They needed everything to be 'normal'.

I phoned our closest family and explained that he was back and that we would be spending time talking and would not like to be disturbed by phone calls. Everyone was very respectful and understanding.

We spent all day talking. It was very intense and for me extremely emotional. The pain was harrowing. There were many tears and much sobbing. Lots of tissues were needed.

That night I was praying and God showed me a picture:

> It was a picture of me placing my husband's wedding ring on
> the coffee table and showing him complete forgiveness.

I cried out to God. I didn't know whether I could do it – *really* forgive him after what he had done! I kept praying and I kept seeing the same picture over and over again. I *knew* that I had to do it. It was so difficult. It was so painful. It was so hard.

Wednesday 24th February 2010

The next day was Wednesday morning. I looked at my husband's wedding finger and noticed that he wasn't wearing his wedding ring. I asked him why and where was it? He told me that he had not been wearing it for weeks but I hadn't noticed. He was right, I hadn't. I had got so used to him taking it off for football that I hadn't noticed. He said that he had been keeping it in his wallet.

I found it strange that it would mean enough to him to take his wedding ring off during his affair with this other woman. If our marriage meant nothing to him, then why bother taking it off at all? Was it a symbol of marriage or guilt? I looked down at my left hand. I loved my wedding rings. I felt really guilty for not noticing. How could I have not noticed?

Later that morning I saw his wallet lying on the side. My heart started beating faster inside my chest. I opened it and found his wedding ring. I took it out of his wallet and put it into my jeans pocket.

I had to trust God. The picture was not going away. I knew in my heart that I had to do what God was asking me to do, no matter how strange, difficult, painful or completely crazy it seemed.

I still remembered what God had spoken to me on the 6th February, when I walked up the steep dark alley, carrying my shopping – before all this began: "Trust in the Lord with all your heart and lean not on your own understanding."

I certainly didn't understand why God would ask me to forgive him now. But I had to try. I was more scared of my husband's reaction than of looking silly.

How could I honestly forgive him? How was that possible? What about all the bare-faced lies he had told me, our children and all our friends and family over the last six months? This was so difficult. I felt emotionally and mentally abused. But the picture of me putting his wedding ring on the coffee table didn't leave me.

Every time I looked at him, all I saw was the man I loved. The man I married, my best friend.

At some point during the day when we were talking, I took his ring out of my pocket. I did what I saw in the picture. My husband was sitting opposite me on the chair in the lounge. I reached out and placed his wedding ring onto the coffee table and said that I forgave him. I told him that I loved him. I said that I wanted him to stay and for us to work it out. I said that he could choose whether to pick it up and put it back on his finger and stay, or not. The choice was his.

Inside our wedding bands we'd had the words engraved: "Forever Yours." Those words meant a great deal to me and so did our wedding rings.

I said that when we got married we had promised that we were "Forever Yours" and that we were meant to be together for ever.

Again I said that I forgave him and I loved him. I loved him so much.

He stood up, got out of the chair, walked over and sat next to me on the couch. He put his arms around me and held me. He cried and we cried together. He said that he was sorry for everything and for causing me so much pain. He said that he had wanted me to find out so many times but he couldn't bring himself to tell me the truth.

I really wanted him to stay. I loved him. He was my best friend. I wanted us to work it out – go to marriage guidance – anything. My heart was so broken.

He kept saying he was not sure whether he was going to stay or leave. That hurt a great deal. There was nothing I could do. I couldn't 'make' him stay. I couldn't say anything to him that would convince him to stay. I was so very upset. I felt as if I was being dangled on a string – kept in limbo – I had no security. I felt so betrayed and confused. Why would there even be a decision to make? How difficult could it be? We had been together for so many years. How could he decide to leave?

I was simply in a place of 'waiting' over the next few days; waiting for a decision from him – to stay – or to leave. It was a decision only he could make. I had not 'told' him what to do. I didn't kick him out at the first sight of him.

I wanted the decision to be his. I loved him. But the scary thing was that I had absolutely no idea what his decision would be. I had doubts that he would leave but I never once seriously thought he would.

All I kept thinking about was the children. How much it would break their hearts if he left? What would we do? What would I do? How would I cope if he left? Us separated? Surely not!

Often when I asked him a question about the affair, he would not answer straightaway. He would remain silent for a very long time. Many minutes would pass before he would utter a word. It wasn't an angry, arms-crossed silence, but he would just sit there with his eyes looking at his lap saying nothing. It was so irritating. But the more I asked, the more silent he became. So I decided to wait patiently for his answers. It was so incredibly annoying and unnecessary but I remained completely calm at all times and waited.

I wanted answers to my questions. I didn't want him to squirm out of answering them. So I waited, mostly in tears.

On the Wednesday evening, the children knew that something was very wrong. We tried to be as normal as we could but, that evening, my youngest daughter said: "Dad, it's nice you having dinner with us. You haven't had dinner with us for ages."

At this point, he walked into the kitchen and paced frantically. He could hardly contain himself. He was pacing, fidgeting and close to tears. What she said was completely true. He hadn't been home for dinner for many weeks. Even she at ten years old had noticed. It didn't seem to matter when I had confronted him over it for the past few months, but when she stood there and said those few words, the truth hit home.

As she came into the kitchen, she said: "Dad, what's wrong? Why are you sad?"

Struggling to speak, staring at the kitchen work surface, he replied: "Nothing's wrong."

But she was insistent. She kept on with the same question. When our other two children came home from their activities later that evening, she asked him again and again. She wouldn't let it drop.

As he sat on the couch, he started to cry.

We were all looking at him now. I sat on the chair, but I didn't move. I couldn't move. This was all up to him. He had to be the one to speak, not me.

All the children started to gather around him. They were all saying at once, "What's wrong, Dad?" "What is it?" "Why are you crying?"

Tears stung my eyes. Then, while still crying, he said, "I'm sorry."

He explained as gently and carefully as he could that he didn't love Mummy any more and that he might be moving out. He said he had been seeing another lady in London, and he was sorry for not being home much lately, and for lying to them.

Their eyes were getting bigger and bigger and they started crying and sobbing. You could see they were in shock. *My Dad?* Doesn't love Mummy? Leaving? They wrapped their arms around him.

It was a moment I would never want to see repeated in my lifetime. It was really heartbreaking. We had not planned to talk to the children at that point but it just happened in that moment. It was so incredibly painful. To witness my children crying and sobbing and clinging onto him was so emotional. All I wanted to do was to wrap my arms around each of them.

But there was nothing I could do. I was helpless. I had tried my best. I hoped in my heart that he would stay. I didn't think for one moment he would actually leave. My son walked out of the room after a few minutes and slammed his bedroom door.

We explained to the children that we would continue to talk about it and let them know very soon. We said that Dad was home for the rest of that week, and we would be spending the next few days talking about it.

Friday 26th February 2010

On the Friday my husband and I went for a walk around a local lake while the children were at school. I had no idea what his decision was going to be, but I felt very afraid.

We stopped for lunch in the café. As I was eating my cake, he said the words that would change my life for ever. He said that he had decided to leave. Just like that! It was over. Everything was finished. He didn't love me any more. He hadn't loved me for a long time. He would be moving out.

I was taken by surprise. I put my fork down, instantly losing my appetite. I couldn't speak for a few seconds. I couldn't believe it. *That's it? Over?* What were the last four days for? All that talking and crying. *For what?*

I felt so angry and hurt. *All that talking seemed so pointless.* I sat there in a room full of people, and I felt so alone. I didn't know what to say. I felt stupid for thinking he would stay. I felt as if the last few days of complete and utter agony had been for nothing. What was it all about anyway? I had tried to be a good person. I had tried to give him time to make his decision. Now it felt as if he had made it long ago.

Just like that! Nothing! No attempt to try to repair the damage caused. No attempt to try to 'work it through'. Nothing! Our marriage was over!

Who was this woman? What did she have that we didn't have? I couldn't understand that he would throw away nearly twenty years together for another woman.

I could not believe that he was going to tell our children that he would be moving out!

It seemed so unbelievable and I was completely unprepared for his answer. I looked around me. The café was quite busy; people bustling about, ordering lunch, getting cutlery and napkins. One couple sat opposite our table. I looked at them briefly. I felt so deflated, so sad and looked down at my plate.

So many thoughts ran around my head. How could this be happening to me? I didn't understand. How could he walk out on his wife and three children? It must take incredible self-indulgence to do that. I know I couldn't do it. How could he? I felt so worthless in that moment, devalued, small and rejected. I was suddenly cast aside, feeling meaningless, insignificant and very unloved.

I looked up at him and said very quietly, "We will tell the children in the morning." I didn't feel the need for any stress that evening. It had been too much already.

"You can stay for up to two weeks until you find a place to live," I said. He didn't seem in a rush to leave that day. This in itself seemed weird. Why would he want to stay another moment? Why did he not want to go straight to HER? Nevertheless, he agreed to stay and we agreed that together we would tell the children in the morning.

I hardly slept that night. I couldn't believe that he had decided to leave. I didn't understand it. My head was spinning. What does this mean? What will I do? What would we do? How would it work?

I think I was secretly hoping that he would change his mind by the morning. Nothing had prepared me for the feeling of sheer dread sitting in my stomach; the fear of telling the children, the fear of my husband moving out, the fear of being alone. I kept thinking: I can't do this. I can't! Single parent – me? I couldn't believe it! There was no way I could cope.

I had relied on my husband over the years for so many things, little things. We had just settled into 'our roles'. How on earth was I going to cope without him? I hadn't been on my own for nearly twenty years. Where would we live? How would we cope financially? I only work part-time. That was always our choice when we had our children. We had made a decision that I would work for my own 'pocket money', just a few hours a week, which would mean that I would be home for the children.

Dropping down to one wage when we had our first daughter always seemed the right decision. We didn't have a lot of money, but money wasn't our focus. We got by. But now I lay there, unable to sleep, I questioned all these things. Everything seemed a mess. I felt so afraid, so afraid of our future as a family. The thought of telling the children caused tears to roll down the bridge of my nose onto my pillow.

Saturday 27th February 2010

The next morning was Saturday. Exactly seven days since I found the love letter in his desk drawer.

We woke up and got dressed and gathered the children in the lounge. I was determined that he would be the one to tell the children the truth from his own lips. Not mine. This was his doing. He was their Dad. He had to be the one to tell them the truth.

The children knew something was going on when we called a family meeting.

As we all sat down, all eyes were looking at him. He sat there and told the children the truth. He said that he had decided to move out. He repeatedly told them that he loved them and that he would always be their Dad, and he would see them regularly.

I sat there quietly in the chair, staring at him intently, tissues in my hand. My legs curled up underneath me. I was too afraid to speak. I believed that he had to do this without me uttering a word. I was determined not to do it for him. He had to face up to what he had done and tell our children what he had decided to do next, as it was going to change our lives drastically and with immediate effect. I felt so helpless; tears in my eyes.

I felt as if I had lost and the other woman had won.

I had tried my best to do things right: to be the best wife and mother I could. I told him I loved him and wanted him to stay.

When he had finished speaking, I said in front of the children, "I love Daddy very much and I have forgiven him. I want Daddy to stay, but it's Daddy's choice."

My eldest daughter turned to him and pleaded "Daddy, Mummy forgives you, please stay."

He just sat there looking down at the floor, hands in his lap, fidgeting. He closed his eyes and slowly shook his head.

It was utterly heartbreaking. What was I hoping for in that moment? I truly believed he would stay. I looked at him, tears welling up in my eyes. My heart was shattered into little pieces. I wanted to run over to our children and wrap my arms around them and protect them from all of this pain, but I couldn't move. The grief was overwhelming.

I felt as if I was 'nothing' to him, nothing at all. He broke my heart. It was like a bad dream, except this wasn't a dream at all. I wasn't about to wake up, I was already awake. It was so painful.

My eldest daughter looked at her Dad in bewilderment with big, desperate eyes. But as she looked at her Dad, tears started to pour down her face. She begged him not to leave. But he didn't change his mind. He didn't say he would stay. He kept saying he was sorry and crying.

My son yet again got up and walked out of the room, slamming the door of his bedroom shut. My youngest daughter started to cry.

The children were so very devastated. It was overwhelming to witness. It took a while for the reality to sink in. Their Dad didn't love Mummy any more. Their Dad loved another woman. Their Dad had been lying to everyone for months and he said he was sorry for that; but their Dad was leaving!

They kept pleading with him to stay. It was no good. He told them he loved them and would always love them. He said that he would always be their Dad and would see them often. My husband cried and cried. The girls wrapped their arms around him and everyone sobbed. My eldest daughter came over to me and I held her tight. We cried together.

As I look back now, I am so glad that I didn't let him off the hook. I knew that he had to tell our children himself. It was the best it could be for everyone. All lies were exposed and out in the open. They didn't hear it from someone else. They heard it directly from him, their Dad.

They couldn't blame me. They couldn't blame themselves. They knew the blame fell at Daddy's feet. Nothing was hidden; no more secrets and lies. It was all down to him. He had lied. He was a liar. But he loved them. He was still their Dad.

I believe this has contributed massively to our individual and family healing.

They certainly did not like to hear the truth. This truth caused them and all of us much pain. But they can never look back and ask themselves the question, "Was it my fault? Did I do something to make Daddy leave?"

From that very moment they were free from any feeling of guilt. This was not their fault. This had nothing to do with them. They needed it to be clear and simple. Their Dad had been having an affair, which was very wrong. He no longer loved Mummy. He loved this 'other woman' instead. He was leaving. This was his choice. He refused to stay. He loved them very much. He would see them often.

After a while, he came over to my chair and put his arms around me and said, "You are the strongest person I know."

Strong? That was not me! I was a complete wreck! My world had fallen apart. I was not strong at all! "I'm not very strong," I whispered, teary-eyed, voice shaking. How could he look at me and say that I was the strongest person he knew? It almost felt as if my being strong gave him the excuse to leave me.

"Yes, you are," he replied.

I have always remembered that. It made me feel cheap. Almost as if he had convinced himself that I would be 'fine'. I didn't feel fine. My life was in turmoil. My life had just collapsed in one week. The man I loved with all my heart didn't love me any more and was leaving. Everything I knew that was secure around me was crumbling. The family we had built up together was being ripped apart. I couldn't stand up. I stayed in that chair for a long time, crying and sobbing.

A little while later I phoned my work and spoke to my boss. I had to tell her what had happened and that I couldn't possibly go to work. I picked up the phone and dialled her number. The moment I had to explain what had happened, the tears started falling and the words stuck in my throat. It was such a difficult phone call, but I knew that it was essential.

My boss was so gracious, kind and understanding. I was so very grateful to her. She gave me a couple of weeks off straightaway. I knew that I would need it. I also knew that I had to focus on the next few days. As I put the phone down, I cried.

Chapter 6: 7 Days of Purpose

Being Practical

Sunday 28th February 2010

I got up on Sunday morning after another sleepless night. I went downstairs. It was early. Everyone was still asleep.

I closed the lounge door and sank to my knees. I prayed. I poured my heart out to God. I didn't know what else to do. All I could do was pray. I *had* to trust God.

I needed God so desperately to help me; to save my marriage.

> *(Psalm 71)*
> *(1) In you, O Lord, do I put my trust and confidently take refuge; let me never be put to shame or confusion! (2) Deliver me in Your righteousness and cause me to escape; bow down Your ear to me and save me! (3) Be to me a rock of refuge in which to dwell, and a sheltering stronghold to which I may continually resort, which You have appointed to save me, for You are my rock and my Fortress. (4) Rescue me, O my God, out of the hand of the wicked, out of the grasp of the unrighteous and ruthless man. (5) For You are my hope; O Lord God, You are my trust from my youth and the source of my confidence. (Amplified Bible).*

That scripture meant a great deal to me. I read it a few times. I cried and cried. I prayed and 'put my trust' in God. I believed with all my heart that God was my 'Rock,' my 'Stronghold,' my 'Fortress.' I prayed that God would 'rescue' me. I knew that God was 'my hope'.

I prayed for a long time. After I had prayed I felt a peace in my heart. I knew that God was with me, helping me.

After I finished praying, I found a pad of A4 paper and a pen. I sat down and started writing.

My husband and I had agreed when we'd had lunch the previous day that he would stay a maximum of two weeks, to give him time to find a flat. It may sound utterly crazy, but it seemed the best thing for our family at the time.

I said that I would help him to find a flat and that we would visit properties and estate agents together.

I told him before he moved out that there were jobs that he needed to do first.

I went straight into organising mode and list-writing. There were two pages by the time I had finished.

As I look back now, some of the things on the list seem quite ridiculous and unnecessary, but at the time they seemed crucial.

There were things like: clear out the shed in the back garden; sort out the bills; help me to understand the bills, and show me what our incomings and outgoings were. We were to go to a stationery shop to purchase files, spreadsheet books, pens, paper, highlighters, etc. I also wanted to sort out what maintenance he would pay me to cover all the household bills. He had to phone all the utility companies to change them into my name.

I also made appointments for us to go to the bank together to discuss our mortgage; visit estate agents and solicitors.

The most important thing we did during this time was to sit down together and draw up a Separation Agreement. This was not legally binding but together we agreed how much maintenance he would provide, and it gave me peace of mind not only for my future but also for the children's. Also on the 'to do' list was for me to purchase myself a new bed, complete with new linen and accessories. This was to be my largest and most essential purchase.

As soon as he told me he would be moving out, my first thought was that I needed a new bedroom – 'new' being the key word. New *everything*! Out with the old and in with the new. The thought of my husband sleeping with another woman and climbing into our bed over the last six months made me feel sick to the stomach! I didn't want anything to remind me of that!

I decided to buy the bed I wanted. It sounds rather trivial, but it felt really good to choose exactly what *I* wanted. The day I spoke to the assistant and placed my order I burst into tears – right there in the shop! I didn't mean to cry. I looked fine when I walked in to the department, yet when I opened my mouth to speak, I cried instead.

After this I walked out onto the high street feeling pretty proud of myself. I had managed it. My new bed would be arriving on the 11th March. That meant that I would have five days after my husband planned to move out to redecorate my bedroom completely.

There was a lot to do. We completed the list in five days. Those five days were very busy.

One of the most difficult things for me to grasp was the finances. All the years we had been together, my husband had dealt with every aspect of our finances.

It was incredibly daunting to have the weight of the finances suddenly resting on my shoulders. I can't stress enough just how difficult it was for me to try to get my head around all those figures. It did not come easily to me at all. I am not mathematical. I had never had to pay bills or to phone companies regarding finance. It was a steep learning curve and it was scary.

But I knew that before my husband walked out of the house, I would have to have control of my finances and know every single detail about them.

First I had to have the right stationery. So we went to the shops to buy everything I needed to get started. It sounds ridiculous, but the biggest challenge for me was to decide 'how' to do my bills. I didn't want to use the computer in case my computer crashed. So I opted for writing everything on paper and filing it.

Next I wanted to make sure that I saved each month for 'everyday' bills such as food and petrol and those bills that recur on a regular basis: birthdays, Christmas, holidays, children's school clothes, car tax, MOT and servicing for the car. I spent a long time in the shop with my husband trying to figure out what items to purchase that would allow me to record all these things. We then sat the table together later that day, working it all out.

Looking back, I'm not sure now what exactly I was afraid of. But as time has passed, I am so very glad that I faced the challenge head on and dealt with it at the time.

It took a great deal of effort to go through the paperwork, to understand what my outgoings and incomings were. It was the one area I did not want to overlook or bypass – I am a meticulous person and I not only wanted to understand the figures, but to manage them without fear.

It was also important to me that I should try to be a good steward of our finances. Therefore, I planned to tithe my income, which means giving ten per cent to my local church.

God taught me so much during that time. I am so grateful to God. I remember the first cheque I wrote out in April as a single parent. It was exactly ten per cent of my earnings. I gave it with a cheerful heart. I have tithed my income for a long time and I was not about to stop. I have not once held back on giving to God first. I believe that through this, God has blessed me and my family in so many ways.

We also discussed at length the issue of childcare. We came to an agreement on what days my husband would see the children and we each purchased a calendar and spent a whole afternoon working out dates. I hung it on the kitchen wall so that the children could instantly see what days they would be going to their Dad. This was positive and encouraging for them.

It's funny but those five days were almost fun! In between the busyness we would stop for lunch and sit and laugh together – it was completely bizarre. We went to visit properties and probably appeared to the estate agent to be a happily married couple. I was determined to go with him to choose the right flat in which my children would be staying. It was a good decision.

I didn't want anything to remain 'hidden' – no more secrets. I wanted everything to be out in the open. I wanted us to go through everything together and make decisions together.

The Bible says, "There is nothing impossible for God." I believe that God helped me greatly over those two weeks. That may sound completely crazy to someone else, but I didn't plan it that way, it seemed to happen that way.

I would have found it completely unbearable if my husband had walked into the house from his holiday, gathered his belongings and left. I seriously don't know what would have happened if I had put his clothes in bags outside, or screamed and shouted when he walked through the front door.

Instead of reacting with my emotions, I had to rely on God to help me to walk in God's love and forgiveness. I can honestly say that I do not regret keeping in step with God's love. The abundant blessings that God has poured out over our family since this time has been truly remarkable.

Those two weeks took all of my courage, strength and determination. I gave every ounce of myself into making it work. I still had to be Mum. I still had three children to look after.

I look back now and I am amazed at how I managed to get through each day. The truth is that it was so much better for me to remain focused on preparing myself as much as I could, before he left.

I was determined that he would not walk out of the door, leaving me in a mess.

It paid off.

There was no anger. There was no malice, bitterness, hatred or un-forgiveness: only love.

It was all God. God enabled me to get through it. God enabled me to love my husband, to love the unlovable.

Chapter 7: Abandoned

In Shock and Alone

> *1 Corinthians 7:13-15*
> *(13) And if a woman has a husband who is not a believer and he is willing to live with her, she must not divorce him. (14) For the unbelieving husband has been sanctified through his wife, and the unbelieving wife has been sanctified through her believing husband. Otherwise your children would be unclean, but as it is, they are holy. (15) But if the unbeliever leaves, let him do so. A believing man or woman is not bound in such circumstances; God has called us to live in peace.*

I became a Christian in 2001 after completing an Alpha course. I had always gone to Church intermittently over the years. I was confirmed in my early twenties in my local Anglican church. But then, quite by accident, in September 2000 I found myself attending an Alpha course at a local Baptist church. Since then, I have discovered that there was nothing accidental about it. God had a plan.

A few weeks beforehand, my two friends and I were sitting at a table in our Mother and Toddler group. It was a Thursday morning. One of my friends who was a Christian, went around the entire hall asking people if they were interested in attending the course.

My friend and I were not. When our other friend rejoined us at the table, I asked, "Did you get anyone to go on your course?"

"No," was her reply.

I felt really sorry for her. After exchanging glances with my two friends, I said, "Well, if you go on it, I will too." So, it was as simple as that. A few weeks later, we sat in a dusty old church hall, in very old squishy chairs listening to talks about Alpha. It was all quite unexpected.

In the next few months both my friend and I became Christians. The day that I became a Christian, God completely changed my life. A few years later, again, completely unplanned, we were both baptised on the same day. Isn't God marvellous!

Sadly, my husband was not a Christian. Over the years the faith that he held from his childhood into his teenage years seemed to fade into the distance and disappear altogether. He later professed not to believe in God at all.

The scripture above is one that I held onto especially during those 7 Days of Purpose.

I knew in my heart that I had to let my husband make his own decision. It was important that that was his decision. I tried my best to convince him that we could work it through. I talked until I ran out of things to say. But I knew that this scripture was saying that I had to let him leave if he so chose.

I have been over and over this scripture many times. What good would it have done to make him stay?

Saturday 6th March 2010

The day had arrived.

The children helped their Dad pack the last few boxes into his car.

He came into the lounge and sat down. It was so emotional. There were tears from the children. Then I started to cry. We chatted for a few minutes. I told him I loved him and wanted him to stay. He said he had to leave.

He hugged the children and told them that he loved them and would be seeing them soon. I sat in the chair and cried. He came over to me and hugged me.

After a very emotional few minutes, he walked out of the front door. It was totally devastating!

It was two weeks to the very day since I found the love letter.

It was almost unreal. It felt as if he had just gone to the shops and would be back in a minute. It was really horrible.

Our lives would never be the same again. They changed in that very moment for ever. In a moment of his choosing, everything we had created together was destroyed; once a very ordinary, carefree and loving family, now suddenly thrown into the pit of the unknown. Separation!

My expectations that we would always be a family together, halted; my hopes and dreams of spending our lives together, forever shattered, lying in ruins at my feet. I was full of fear and dread. It consumed me. It was like a dream. Everything felt numb. I couldn't think any more. I could not believe he was walking out of the door. I could not believe he was walking out on us. We were his family. We loved him. How could he leave?

My heart was broken. As he walked out of the front door, it made its usual clicking sound behind him.

I will always remember the details of these few days. When the front door closed behind him, the house was strangely peaceful. I curled up in the chair. All of a sudden, I noticed the sun streaming through the window, light filling the room. My two youngest children ran to the sofa and clambered as high as they could to wave to him from the window. My eldest daughter ran upstairs to her bedroom. We watched his car drive off down the road.

The children were very calm. It was as if Dad was going on holiday. After a few minutes they got down from the sofa and went to their bedrooms. The house was extraordinarily still. No-one spoke. The children shed a few tears but everything was peaceful.

After a little while, I got up and walked upstairs. I put my head around the door of my eldest daughter's bedroom. My heart broke further. She was sitting on her window-sill, tears pouring down her face. I went into her room and put my arms around her. She cried and cried.

Afterwards I walked very quietly into my bedroom. I pulled back the duvet and got into bed. I lay my head on the pillow and pulled the duvet over my head. I quietly cried and cried.

About half an hour later my youngest daughter came into my bedroom and whispered worriedly, "Mummy?" I couldn't speak. I couldn't move. She walked round to the other side of the bed and got in beside me. She looked into my eyes. She held my hand. I wrapped my arms around her. I hugged my daughter for what seemed like ages.

I remember that moment as if it were yesterday. It still brings tears to my eyes even now. It was the saddest day in my life. There are some moments which just seem to 'catch' me out. That day was so very painful. Just like that, my husband walked out on our marriage; on me, on us.

I felt betrayed; completely abandoned, rejected, thrown away and discarded. I was on my own.

It was his choice to leave.

I did not throw him out. I hadn't told him to leave. I asked him to stay – and he chose to leave.

He was not the slightest bit interested in trying to work things out. He had made up his mind and he had left.

It took me a long time to come to terms with that: to know that the man I had married and had been with for twenty years could think so little of me, that he could leave and not at least 'try' to make our marriage work.

But the decision was not mine to take. It was solely his.

He chose to walk out of the front door because he didn't love me any more, and was in love with another woman.

He had no consideration for me – for his wife, for our children. It seemed our feelings did not matter. In our own way, each of us felt as if we were less important to him than this other woman.

How can that be? How can a man suddenly walk out of the family home in pursuit of life with another woman and leave behind his wife and children without a second glance?

I will never understand that decision. At the time, all I could think was that we could just … try.

But I wasn't worth trying for. I felt like nothing. I felt the most worthless person on the planet. I was left behind. I was so intensely sad. If we had no children then maybe I would never have seen him again. Who knows?

But this I do know – the pain was so unbearable that it is almost indescribable.

Our marriage was defiled. Our marriage was over – finished – non-existent from that moment.

It seemed to me that everything we had worked for over the years seemed futile, worthless and unimportant to him.

The damage was mental and emotional. The children lost faith in their Dad that day. Their trust in their Dad was destroyed. I'm not convinced that they will ever trust him completely again. He let them down. He walked out. He didn't try to repair the damage he had caused. Instead he left. He chose to hug us all and say goodbye.

The children and I were hurt a great deal that day. It was unspoken hurt, too deep to talk about at the time, deep-rooted pain, scarring the soul. That day will always be imprinted on my memory. I can still see him going out of the front door, climbing into his car, putting on his seatbelt and waving at us as he drove off.

I wrote in my diary that evening:

> Today was really painful, it was really difficult. I didn't want him to leave. I told him how much I loved him and how much I wanted him to stay.
>
> He didn't ask to stay … or say that he wanted to work things out. I felt as if I wasn't 'worth' fighting for. I had lost.
>
> I know that I have to trust God despite how things may appear – despite the circumstances surrounding us.

It must be so devastating for children to watch their Dad pick up his belongings and walk out of the door because he loves another woman. The damage is irreparable. Trips to the cinema, outings, money, holidays, etc. would never be enough to repair such damage.

The pain the children have felt has been displayed in all sorts of ways.

> *Psalm 6:3-6 (NIV) says:*
> *(3) "My soul is in anguish. How long, O Lord, how long?" (4) Turn,*
> *O Lord, and deliver me; save me because of your unfailing love … (6)*
> *I am worn out from groaning; all night long I flood my bed with*
> *weeping and drench my couch with tears.*

Those scriptures really spoke to me that day. My soul was in complete anguish. I had been going through this turmoil for so long. I had been living in a house where the atmosphere was so tense and on edge. I cried out to the Lord with the exact words from the Psalm: "*How long Lord, how long?*"

I believe that Jesus Christ died on the cross for my sins. I prayed that God would indeed 'turn to me; deliver me, and save me'. I certainly felt utterly 'worn out from groaning', and 'weeping'; and for many nights my pillow had been drenched with tears.

The Bible says that God loves us with an 'unfailing love'. My husband didn't love me; that was very clear. But I clung onto the fact that God *did* love me. God's love was much stronger. God's love was 'unfailing'. God's love would never fail.

Unfailing means continuous or reliable. God's love is boundless. It is endless, persistent and certain. God is faithful.

In other words, the Bible showed me that God's love was a love that I could rely and depend upon. It would never end. It was real.

I needed to read that Psalm that very evening. It was so comforting to know that God loved me regardless.

When my husband walked out, I felt so very much unloved. I was rejected by the one person in the world I loved and treasured. I also lost my best friend.

I was abandoned. My children felt abandoned, although they knew that they would be seeing their Dad soon. That gave them some comfort. He was not deserting them completely but they were distraught nonetheless.

And all for what? His own selfish desires, his own needs, his own wants. In other words, it was all for 'himself'. He chose to put himself first before anyone else.

Heartless.

Selfish.

After I had stayed in bed for a long time I got up and got everyone ready. That Saturday evening was our Church event and I was determined to go.

Maybe I am the craziest person. Maybe he was right when he said that I was the strongest person. Maybe I *was* strong.

But then I had God on my side. God loved me. I wanted to go to that event for only one reason: I had been looking forward to it. We got ready and left the house at 5pm.

It was only a few hours since he had left.

At the end of the evening the leadership team of the church were asked to come forward to make a prayer tunnel to pray for people. A prayer tunnel is two lines of people forming an arch with their hands and praying for people as they walk through it. This particular evening it took over an hour for everyone to pass through and be prayed for.

I sat there not knowing what to do. I was a leader. I remember silently praying, standing up and asking God to help me. I asked God to use me in some way. I told Him that I felt completely useless and unable to pray with people at that moment. I only stood up out of obedience.

I didn't want to go up to the front. My thoughts were racing. All I kept thinking was that I couldn't pray for people. Not me! Help me, Lord!

I stood opposite one of the Church elders. We formed a long prayer tunnel. We were the last pair.

God showed me something amazing that evening. As people started to come through, we would pray for them. God gave me incredible words for each person. For nearly everyone that came past, God gave me a word. It was amazing. I knew that it was certainly not me. I had no strength and I had nothing to give anyone.

As I began to speak out what God was showing me, I felt so much compassion for each person. I wanted God to use me, somehow; and God did!

No-one would have known what I had gone through only a few hours beforehand. I was simply a leader being obedient. I didn't refuse to go forward. I didn't say I couldn't do it. I trusted in God.

Afterwards, the elder opposite me said to me: "You are a person walking in victory! You displayed victory." Wow! Me? Displaying victory? I certainly didn't feel as if I was victorious in any shape or form. In fact, I felt quite the opposite. As I tried to take in those words, the tears poured down my face. As I stood there, I knew that God had clearly been using me. I didn't think God could use me when I was so broken. I felt as if I had nothing to offer anyone.

I wrote in my diary that evening:

> The Church Elder was right. I hadn't thought that about myself, me – 'displaying victory'. But when he said it, I felt joy and strength rise up in my heart. I love Jesus. I believe Jesus has a greater plan than I can imagine. God is so awesome!

Sunday 7th March 2010

The next morning was Sunday, the day after my husband had moved out. It was the day before his birthday.

I woke up feeling very alone and yet peaceful. It was a strange feeling. I had no anxiety or dread sitting in my stomach any more. That had gone. Neither did I have fear going around in my head.

The house was really quiet. No-one else seemed to be awake.

I felt very lost and still quite numb.

Then thoughts started bombarding my mind. 'Where was he? What was he doing? Was he having a good time? I wasn't! How could he do this to me? Did our marriage mean nothing to him?'

I didn't understand it at all. I couldn't process what it all meant.

What was he doing? As I lay in bed, all I could think was: 'Why?'

I felt trapped. How could he just walk out on our family? My head was buzzing with questions. I didn't feel stressed but I felt so incredibly sad. I felt lost. His stuff was gone. He wasn't here.

He had dropped all his responsibilities at the front door! It broke my heart.

What made it worse was that we had made a promise to our children. We had promised each of them that we would be their 'forever family'.

All three of our children are adopted. We adopted each of them individually over a ten-year period.

When I was nineteen I found that I couldn't have children. I was lying on a hospital bed at the time. My best friend was with me. The doctor stood to the side of the bed and spoke in a very matter-of-fact voice. He told me what was wrong, and then said, very bluntly, that I would never be able to have children.

It was heartbreaking. But even in those early days I made an inward decision. I decided that one day I would adopt children.

I told my husband this before we got married, and even then I carried a strong determination that I would adopt at some point.

We approached Social Services at the early stages of our marriage. We were told we had to wait four years before we could apply, due to the fact that we were so young, and that we hadn't been married very long. That didn't worry us. We were happy to wait.

When the four years were up, we approached them again. We went through the initial interviews, group courses, medicals and home visits, and completed all the forms.

From the very beginning we were always open and honest about who we were as people; our past, and our hopes and dreams for the future. We didn't hold anything back. We just went with it. The process was quite daunting, intimidating, personal, emotional and challenging, but we got through it together.

We adopted our eldest daughter when she was nearly two years old. I still remember the day clearly. We drove to the foster parents' house to visit her for the first time. As we pulled into the street, there she was. The front door of the house was wide open. Inside the doorway stood a woman holding the hands of a little girl who was standing in front of her. The girl stood there smiling, with pigtails in her hair. She looked utterly adorable. I fell in love with her at that very moment and I hadn't even got out of the car!

There she was! My little girl! My baby! We both grinned from ear to ear as we walked up the driveway.

That first meeting was nerve-racking, but we could not stop smiling. In all the photos, there we are with those big grins on our faces.

Three years later, it all happened again. This time, three of us were in the car. Our daughter had her favourite dress on. She was so excited to be going to meet her 'new' sister for the first time. We had been talking about it for weeks.

Getting out of the car, we held her hands as we walked towards the front door. We knocked nervously and one of the foster parents answered the door. We were invited into the lounge. There she was! Our second daughter, sitting on the floor playing with her toys. She was beautiful!

She was nearly two. Our eldest daughter was nearly five. We were all so happy to meet her. The girls got on so well together.

Then, when our eldest daughter was nearly eight and our youngest daughter was nearly five, we adopted our youngest daughter's brother. He was nearly seven years old.

Two weeks later we all went on holiday. I remember it so clearly. The holiday had been booked and was quite local, so we didn't have to go far. When we adopted the girls, we stayed at home for a couple of weeks and introduced the family to them slowly. But with our son, it all happened so quickly and unexpectedly that we almost had to fit him into our existing routine.

We made the decision to go on holiday and take one day at a time. It worked really well. When we got to the hotel, we spoke to some of the other guests. One of the girls mentioned their 'new brother'. The man to whom she had made the comment looked rather puzzled so we explained that we had only just adopted our son a few weeks before.

Towards the end of that week, that same man came up to me. He said he would never have thought that our son had only been with us for a few weeks. He said that he looked as if he had been part of the family for ever.

That was a comment that made us smile. Yes, that man was right. We were a family. We all had a fabulous time.

Each adoption process was tough, really tough. In fact, just because we had gone through the process once before, it didn't make the second time any easier. When it came to adopting the third time, the process was even more gruelling. Each adoption contained numerous forms to fill in, and endless visits from social workers.

When we applied to go through that third adoption process, our eldest daughter was at school and our youngest was at nursery. Our social worker set up appointments and interviews with both the nursery and the school's teachers. This time we had to provide six referees.

The adoption process was time-consuming and life-consuming. It seemed to take over every aspect of our daily lives with meetings, assessments and paperwork constantly being squeezed into the diary. It was a massive family commitment, a serious commitment. It was life-changing.

A big chunk of our marriage was spent going through the adoption process. We were 'adopters' who were 'waiting' to be matched to a child; then having our 'new' child live with us; going through the legal side of the adoption process and being in constant touch with solicitors. After visiting the judge and becoming adoptive parents, we were a new family. Then after a couple of years we started all over again.

I love them each with all my heart. They are my children. They are so incredibly precious and beautiful.

That is what saddens my heart. They had already been through a great deal of their own heartache. They had had their own stories to tell. They had previous lives and experiences before they came to live with us. We were meant to protect them, to be there for them for ever, to love them, to be their new 'forever family' … for ever.

Each of them had been through such a lot already. We made a decision when we adopted our eldest daughter never to talk about their history. It is theirs. It is private. It is not for us to share. It is for them to share, only if they choose to do so. It will always be their decision.

I'm so glad we made that decision. I am so very proud of them. We have always talked very openly and positively about adoption.

I asked my children's permission whether or not I could mention in this book the fact that they are adopted. My eldest said, laughing, "I'm so used to it now, Mum, it's fine." My youngest said rather dramatically, rolling her eyes and smiling at the same time, "It's fine, Mum, really."

So I add it only to give some insight into the far greater depth of sadness we have felt and experienced. They already knew what it is like to be separated from their birth parents and subsequent foster parents. They have had to live with that themselves for many years.

My husband, walking out of our front door, only added to their pain. It was another let-down, another conversation point; another point that needed explaining when speaking to their friends. They have always felt 'different'. They are adopted. Now they are adopted, and their parents are separated.

We were a family of five. Now we were a family of four.

How can we ever trust anyone again?

I glanced at my bedside clock. It would soon be time to get up for church. It was so difficult thinking about everything.

My heart was red-raw; open, bleeding, crushed. I dragged myself out of bed, thanks to the grace of God. I had to get the children up. We had plans. I didn't want to lie there feeling sorry for myself all day – why give my husband the satisfaction of that! He didn't care, he was out enjoying himself – obviously!

No way was I going to allow myself to sink into a pit. I wanted to save my dignity. I *had* to fight for my integrity. I was not going to stay in this bed one more minute!

Regardless of what he was doing at that exact moment, I had to get up and get on with it. I had three children to look after. There was no rest for me.

I wasn't frightened or scared of facing the world as a single parent. That part didn't faze me at all. I was still in shock. Then I had crazy thoughts like: 'Maybe he'll change his mind and come home today?' Crazy, I know, but totally believable while I was lying there. My heart was filled with sadness. Grief overwhelmed my heart. I was alone.

I had just lost my very best friend in the whole wide world. The person I confided in, the person I loved, cherished and trusted more than anyone else. There was a gaping great hole in my heart, in my life, in my house, in my bed.

As I sat up in bed amongst a sea of emotions and thoughts, I picked up my Bible and opened it. I read this Psalm. It brought tears of sorrow and joy.

> *Psalm 73:23-28*
> *(23) Yet I am always with you; you hold me by my right hand. (24) You guide me with your counsel, and afterward you will take me into glory. (25) Whom have I in heaven but you? And earth has nothing I desire besides you. (26)* <u>*My flesh and my heart may fail, but God is the strength of my heart and my portion for ever.*</u> *(27) Those who are far from you will perish; you destroy all who are unfaithful to you. (28)* <u>*But as for me, it is good to be near God. I have made the Sovereign Lord my refuge;*</u> *I will tell of all your deeds.*

God's word said that God was 'always' with me, that God was 'holding me by my right hand'.

I certainly felt that 'my flesh and my heart may fail'. My heart was in tatters. Tears rolled down my cheeks. 'But God is the strength of my heart and my portion for ever.' Wow! God *is* my strength. I desperately needed strength. More than anything, strength was needed. I had to get up and get dressed but it was difficult. I could so easily have hidden my face under the duvet and stayed there all day. But I couldn't allow my emotions to overtake the responsibilities of that day. I had to get up.

As I kept reading that scripture, joy poured into my heart. I began to feel light and not heavy. I started to smile to myself. God was *my* helper. God was *my* friend.

God promises 'perfect peace' to those whose 'mind is steadfast.'

> *You will keep in perfect peace him whose mind is steadfast, because he trusts in you (Isaiah 26:3).*

"God is the strength of *my* heart" (vs 26). He is indeed! God is *my* strength! God is "*my* portion for ever".

At a time when I could have felt so weak, consumed by grief, unable to function – I began to feel victorious! I knew that God was with me. I knew that God had a plan. I couldn't see any of it – but I *knew* God was with me. I believed the scriptures. The Bible says that "Jesus is the way, the truth and the life" (John 14:6).

It also says: "*Be strong and courageous. Do not be afraid or terrified because of them, for the Lord your God goes with you; He will never leave you nor forsake you*" (Deuteronomy 31:6).

How easy it would have been for me to fill my heart with resentment, bitterness, anger, hatred and un-forgiveness. I did have many questions. I did have a broken heart, and a broken marriage, but the scriptures really helped me that morning. Soaking in God's word brought joy to my heart.

I could have woken up feeling angry, screaming at everyone. But I didn't. I could have stayed in bed all day and tried to block out the world – but I didn't. I could have spoken negatively or thought negative thoughts – but I didn't. What was the point of that?

I simply felt alone.

I really did need to get up! Enough with all this thinking!

I had to look after the children and sort out their breakfast. There was no-one else to do it. It was all up to me. I *had* to move. I lay there a little bit longer. I kept having this dialogue in my mind. *It is better to keep myself busy. I have to get up. Somehow,* I had to muster up enough courage and stamina to act 'normal' and be Mummy.

I finally pulled myself out of bed and got up. I got everyone dressed. I made an effort to look nice and put on make-up and fix my hair. I spoke in a gentle voice, and tried to smile.

It was a strange morning: peaceful, no more 'walking on eggshells'; no more 'waiting' for his decision, no more tension in every room in the house; no more 'silences' or 'avoidances of conversation'. There were no more 'bleeps from his phone'. Yes, 'peaceful' is a good word. The house felt quiet.

After breakfast, the children and I left the house and went to church. It was tough, very tough – incredibly tough, but we were surrounded by people who loved us. I felt safe there. I felt loved.

Only a few key people knew the situation. I didn't talk about it to anyone else. I didn't announce it to the crowd. I avoided talking about it. That was great therapy for me. I only kept the information to my closest few friends.

I cried though. As soon as worship started, so did my tears. But I was in the right place. We stood at the back, next to one of my best friends. The children and I were quiet. It was out of character for me to stand at the back. I normally stand in the front row! I always make a point of saying hello to everyone, smiling and chatting. But this day I simply stood at the back, not speaking to anyone. I stood securely next to my wonderful friend. Just one look into her tear-filled eyes made mine fill with tears. We hardly spoke. I am so very grateful to her for being my friend. She just stood there next to me. That is what I needed.

It may seem a little crazy to some, going to church the very next day, but it was essential for me to keep things 'normal'. I have used this word many times but I can't think of a better word to describe it.

Inside, my heart was aching with sorrow and anguish. We had been abandoned, left behind, rejected and discarded.

Regardless, I was determined to stand on my own two feet.

Chapter 8: I Choose to Stand!

...And Not Crumble!

Monday 22nd February 2010

Everything was standing against me. Fear seemed to rack my soul and consume my thoughts. I didn't know what to do. I didn't know how to think.

I was exhausted, mentally drained and on edge.

It was Monday, two days after I had found the love letter in my husband's desk drawer. He had not yet returned home from abroad.

Knock! Knock! Knock!

It was the familiar sound of the front door being pounded. It was 8.30am. As usual, I was running late. How could I be late leaving the house with my youngest daughter *every* morning? We only lived a few minutes' walk away from the school gate! But we seemed to be always hurrying up the hill, passing mummies coming down the hill most mornings.

My very good friend and neighbour always knocked for us. Some mornings we would actually walk up with her and her children but, more often than not, I would shout through the letterbox, "You go on, we're running late!" while frantically getting everything ready to leave the house.

I felt sick. I was on the verge of tears. There was a huge knot in my stomach. *How could I face people?*

I was trying my best to appear normal and hold everything together. I had been up very early and packed the children's school lunches and had got everything ready for their day.

Every movement was an effort. Each word that came out of my mouth needed thought before I spoke. My mind was all over the place. My emotions were wrecked.

I had to pack the children off to school as if nothing had happened. At that time they knew something was wrong after the weekend we had had, even though I really had tried to act 'normal'.

What is 'normal' anyway? It certainly wasn't me that particular morning. I felt anxious, jumpy and close to tears. I felt frightened of what would happen when my husband walked through the door later.

As we walked up to school, I put on a brave face when I reached the playground. I didn't want anyone to talk to me that morning – no-one. Just the thought of someone talking to me made me walk faster.

I was so glad that we were late. The playground was empty. I kissed my daughter, handed her book bag and waved to her as she went into the classroom.

I turned around and walked out of the school gate, and quickly made my way home. I kept my head down and my gloved fingers stuffed into my jacket pockets. I opened the front door and walked into the lounge. The phone rang. I picked it up.

"Hello," I said quietly into the receiver.

"Are you all right?" came the urgent reply. It was my neighbour whom I had sent on her way earlier.

I burst into tears. "No," I said tearfully.

"I'll be right down," she said.

I put the phone down and reached for the tissues. I sat in the chair and I started to cry.

Within seconds, my front door burst open and my neighbour walked in. "What's the matter?" she said. She looked at me anxiously, demanding an explanation.

I sat there, looking at her for a few seconds. I could hardly speak. Tears poured down my face. "My husband's been having an affair," I croaked.

"*WHAT?*" she said. She couldn't believe what she was hearing. I don't know what she was expecting me to say, but it wasn't that! For the last six months I had said nothing to her about it. This was shocking! She knew my husband well. Our children played together all the time.

She gave me a hug. She sat and listened. She made me cups of tea (with too much sugar) and made me drink them. She stayed with me for quite a while.

She was so surprised. I had said nothing; nothing – not one word about the past six months. She was not very happy with me for that, and she was not the only one. But I couldn't have told anyone. I couldn't speak about it aloud!

I had been under tremendous stress for what had seemed like ages. But somehow I had managed to 'contain' it. I seemed to separate it from the reality of my daily life. I kept everything hidden: my fears, worries, feelings and anxieties.

I had been for months praying to God, asking Him what was wrong. Now, that answer had come crashing down all around me and it came with major consequences. My husband had been having an affair and had left. It took great courage to get out of bed every morning, to open the front door and step outside.

There was a big world lurking beyond my driveway. The fear of everything *out there* screamed at me the moment I ventured past the small iron wall that marked the edge of my property. It would have been *far easier* to stay inside!

The moment I stepped out of the safe zone of my little house I felt fearful of what was going to happen next. An unending stream of negative thoughts filled my mind; they did not stop. The best way to describe the effect of those terrible thoughts would be to imagine sticking your hand into a big bowl of treacle.

Imagine trying to get through your day with sticky hands! Everything you touch sticks to you. That is what those thoughts seemed to represent to me. If I had allowed myself to believe them, then I would have carried a negative attitude about myself and my life. So I had to remember the promises of God for me.

The temptation was to believe *that I was a failure; that it was my entire fault; that if only I had listened to God earlier I could have saved my marriage.* Even more thoughts tried to attach themselves to me: *I was useless; I was worthless; I was old and ugly; and no-one would want to talk to me.* I felt embarrassed and humiliated. It was relentless and hideous!

But I decided that I was worth more than those horrid thoughts. I knew that God loved me; it said so in the Bible. Something rose up in my spirit and in my heart. I gripped onto the knowledge that I *was* loved. I *was* precious.

Instead of hibernating in the safety of my duvet, I made a decision to face the world; to venture out *into* it and to overcome the fears that were taunting me. I may have felt worthless but I *knew* that I *was* not worthless. God loved me. God cared for me. God was my Rock on whom I placed my feet, my faith, my life, and my decisions.

I chose to stand on the principles of the Bible and the promises in the Bible. It speaks of healing, wholeness, joy and love. I needed that. God shares His heart with us that He loves us unconditionally and that we are precious in His sight.

Everything that I was experiencing was speaking the exact opposite.

Abandonment had left its searing mark on me, even though I *know* God loves *me* unconditionally. I felt totally rejected, humiliated, lost and confused. But in my inner being I was holding up an invisible placard. I was protesting. No-one except me could see it. It was one which displayed my faith, despite my shaky knees and tear-stained face.

My placard read: *I'm standing – I'm standing – I'm standing!*

It was a battle to stand but I was determined that I would not become a 'victim' here! I was not going to allow myself to make decisions out of anger, hurt, jealousy or rage. I may have felt incredibly inadequate and small, but I had to stop myself from screaming at him when I saw my husband.

To me, being 'a victim' and acting 'the victim' were two different things.

Lunches

Over the next few months my husband and I met for lunch a couple of times in a coffee shop. It felt very strange and awkward at first, but it was a useful way of discussing issues away from the children and on neutral ground.

I found it really difficult to have lunch with 'half a person'! He was my husband, but he *wasn't* my husband. I knew nothing about his life. I didn't want to know anything about his life either. I quickly learned that *he* was not *my* friend – we had a really good time during these lunches and laughed a lot together … but there was a difference. I did not trust him. I believe a friend is someone a person trusts and a friendship is built around it. Even if it is never stated, trust is an underlying factor of any relationship.

I found myself sitting opposite the very man who had destroyed my trust. He had carelessly disregarded it, ripped it to shreds and destroyed it. Trust, I have discovered, is highly valuable and highly respected. It can be taken for granted. Once it has been broken, it changes your perception of the person who broke it. They don't seem to be the same as they were before.

But a lot of good came out of those lunches. The fruit was that we were able to discuss matters openly, frankly, positively and constructively. It led us to be able to talk, quickly and efficiently about issues that arose. There have been many times when my husband has dropped the children off and we have spent time discussing issues over a cup of tea. This has been one of the real benefits of being amicable. As parents, we have kept working together in unity over decisions concerning the children, education, finances and the divorce proceedings.

Sometimes, standing is so difficult. I prayed and asked God to help me and to be with me when I met my husband for lunch; to strengthen me and to help me to walk in love; to help me to speak with kindness and humility; not to be anxious, but to be filled with joy rather than sadness.

Where I gathered the strength from I don't know, but I had strength inside me from somewhere. I rested my whole faith on God's shoulders. Every moment of every day I poured out my heart to God. I had to trust God with my brokenness. I prayed and cried out to God, telling Him all of my fears, desperation and hurts. Only God could carry them. Only God could help me.

I am sure that my strong-willed determination stems from my childhood. I am embarrassed to say that I completely failed my Sixth Form year in every subject except English. I was too busy going out with my friends and having fun. I thought that I would breeze through them, no problem. The harsh reality hit me full in the face the day I opened my exam results letter.

We were standing in the kitchen, my parents and I. It was as if a big black cloud had descended on the room. The light seemed to have faded. They both looked at me. All I could see was pity, disappointment and sadness. I had let them down. I had let myself down. I had failed. I was a failure, an idiot, a complete and utter idiot!

There have been a few life-changing moments in my life. That was most definitely one of them. Inside I was distraught. I didn't stand there and cry. I was too much in shock and I knew in my heart that I would have to put it right. I would never, ever, want to fail again!

No more sitting on the phone for hours with my friends talking about teenage nonsense; no more watching the television instead of doing my homework. After a year of hard work and determination, I opened the new results. There were smiles all round. I had passed everything! It had been the biggest challenge I had faced so far.

Now I was approaching my circumstances with a similar determination. Rather than taking residence in the local library with my study books, I now found myself fighting to stand for success of a different kind.

I was standing for my sanity, my life, my children and my freedom. I was not going to be just a 'survivor' of adultery and abandonment – I wanted more, much more, than that!

I decided to take my life back! I wanted to stand up for peace and love in my home and in my heart.

It wasn't easy. Everything was tempting me to stay at home and not venture outside. But I stood on the principle that I would not be a victim and take on a victim's mentality of 'poor me'.

I deliberately didn't take to my bed. I didn't ask people to take my children to school. I wanted to do that for them. I wanted to make their tea, do the washing, food shopping and household chores. I didn't give up. I refused to give up!

I didn't want my family taking over either. They had enough to deal with in their own lives; they didn't need to take on mine as well. I felt an incredible sense of responsibility resting on my shoulders. It was all down to me now.

I had to find the strength and the courage to stand. It was difficult. I felt battered and bruised. My self-esteem plummeted. My confidence was rocked, knocked and beaten down. But somewhere deep inside of myself I refused to let this destroy my life. I would not be beaten. I would not let my husband's behaviour eradicate my confidence and destroy who I was.

I wrote in my diary almost a year later:

> 9th January 2011:
> Being positive, even when everything is desperately bleak, is possible. It is so helpful to restoring your soul.
>
> Why should I allow myself to sink into some kind of apathetic black hole over a man? I am stronger than that! I refuse to!
>
> I am *going* to succeed in life! I'm not talking success, meaning a career. I mean to *stand up*! Be my own person! Enjoy life! Enjoy my children! Love people around me! Help people around me! I have a family who need me! I have three children who need their Mum! They are my main focus!
>
> I want them to be happy and to excel at school despite our family breakdown! I want them to know that they are loved and are very special. It is my job to ensure that they come out of all of this as strong, loving, caring and successful adults.
>
> God's plan has to be far greater than this mess of a marriage, and the daunting pile of divorce paperwork waiting downstairs for me to complete. It has to be!

A few months after my husband had moved out, I was vacuuming the lounge. I had an hour to get ready for work before my mother-in-law arrived to look after the children.

As I stood holding the handle, I suddenly, without warning, felt overwhelmed with grief. I put my hands over my face and knelt on the floor. I started to sob. I found myself gulping back the tears that were streaming down my face.

As I knelt there, I kept saying to God, "I can't do it, God; I can't, I can't do this any more!" I sobbed and sobbed. I poured my heart out to God in those few moments.

I said to God, "I can't go to work! I can't face it. I can't. I can't! O Lord, please help me!"

My nose was running. Tears were pouring and mascara was streaming down my face. I was desperate. I can't describe the grief in my heart in that moment. It consumed me. My body was racked with grief, sadness, loss, emptiness and heartfelt agony.

I'm not sure how long I sat there on the floor, by the vacuum cleaner. It seemed like a long time.

I had no energy or life in my body. I stayed there hunched over the vacuum.

Going to work seemed an enormous feat. Getting ready for work was strenuous; facing another day of smiling at people seemed suddenly unbearable. *How could I do it? How could I face people?* My heart was aching.

My life, marriage and security had been ripped out from underneath me. The full force of grief seemed to take me over. The pain, agony, sorrow and hurt seemed to come from deep inside my heart.

I cried. I couldn't stop. The pain of the weeks and months rose to the surface from my very soul.

After a while I was suddenly aware of the time. I looked at my watch and realised that my mother-in-law would shortly be arriving.

I panicked. I stood up and looked at my reflection in the mirror. *Look at me,* I thought! I didn't want her to see me in such a state.

I stood for a moment and prayed.

I started to thank God for my job; for what a blessing it had been to me. I asked God to help me to get through the rest of the day and to be the best I could be at work.

I quickly finished the vacuuming. I ran upstairs and spent a few minutes splashing cold water on my face. I was ready just in time. I hoped she would not notice my red eyes.

When she knocked on the door, I opened it and tried my best to be smiley and happy. I knew that my face was slightly blotchy and my eyes were red, but we both said nothing. If my mother-in-law had mentioned it, I know for sure I would not have made it out of the house without the tears starting again.

There have been so many occasions that I have felt on the edge of a waterfall of tears. I have said to people, "I'm fine," only to be dodging the real answer hidden in my heart.

I don't want to walk around being a mess all the time.

So I do try to avoid crying in public, although grief is not always controllable. Grief can take me by surprise. The simplest of things can bring me to tears: seeing an old photo of us together as a family, or going near places that we used to visit, all bring back memories.

Grief is very personal. No-one could tell me when I would feel better or when I should be 'over it'. Grieving is a process; it takes time. Some days have been better than others.

God knows everything I'm feeling. He knows every thought I have, every word I speak, every tear I shed. He knows the emptiness in my heart and the sorrow buried deep within.

God knows it all. God loves me: of that I am certain.

Standing – has taken much effort; probably far more effort than I could have imagined. In order to get up each day and *get on with life,* I had to stand, relying constantly on God for help.

But standing *is* possible.

Chapter 9: 'The Doorstep'

Learning to be Amicable

> *Psalm 17:3*
> *Though you probe my heart and examine me at night, though you test me, you will find nothing; I have resolved that my mouth will not sin.*

The 'doorstep' was really difficult.

After my husband moved out, I suddenly had contact with him only 'on the doorstep'. I went from having a husband to having contact with my husband 'on the doorstep' when it was time to collect or drop off the children.

It was a stark reality: he was not interested in me in the slightest. I was just the facilitator to these meetings.

It seemed to have happened overnight. I was cast aside, no longer 'his' wife. I still felt like his wife. I still wore his wedding rings on my finger. I still had our wedding photos up in the house. Yet I wasn't his wife any more. My role as his wife had vanished.

I felt lost. I now found myself in this new situation as 'door-keeper' and 'administration assistant'.

My new role was to make sure that the children were ready when it was time for him to pick them up, and to open the front door with a smile when he dropped them off. I also put his post in a pot inside the porch door.

The conversations were now reduced to discussing the arrangements for the children. I knew nothing of his life. It was horrible. I had been with him for 20 years and now found myself on unfamiliar ground. He wasn't interested in my life. We had nothing to say to one another. It made me feel so isolated and frustrated with him. It was really painful, hurtful and heartbreaking.

That is when we started to become agitated with each other. There was no room for 'normal' conversation; just 'hello' and 'goodbye', which, at best, was mostly muttered.

I very quickly came to feel intimidated, unimportant and like a spare part. I stared at him; he stared down at the front doorstep. Words were difficult to muster. Conversation was limited. I continued to glare at him and he persisted in avoiding eye contact. It became more and more difficult as the days and weeks went by. Those first few instances were horrendous! We started getting really annoyed at one another. On occasion, we shouted at each other, which was really out of character. It became stressful for everyone.

I felt intimidated, not only by his cold demeanour, but by the whole scenario. I worried about what I looked like; what I would say or not say; whether I should smile or ignore him. I worried: *do I open the door or do I let the children use their keys? Do I stand on the doorstep or go and sit on the couch?* It caused me great anxiety.

I felt about as important as the curtains. I still wanted to chat about things as though he still lived there, but I couldn't.

In those early days I felt so mad at him. Even the noise of the car door slamming on the driveway would start my heart pumping. I felt instantly tense, on edge and nervous.

Then, when I would open the front door, the feeling would intensify. Even to look at him filled me with so much pain. *How could he have left me? How could he have lied to me? How could he have slept with another woman? Who was he?* He didn't seem like the same person any more. He was completely detached, always looking at his feet, fidgeting, yet oddly reserved and quietly spoken. It infuriated me!

We had planned a future together! Nothing was the same! It felt so unfair that I found myself in this position. He was all smiles with the children and he was polite to me, but he did not act like 'my husband'. *I felt as if I was nothing.*

I had to pray. I had to seek God. Each time, I prayed before I opened the front door. I asked God to help me to know what to say and how to *be*.

When the children were being dropped off I was determined to open the door with a smile and kiss the children as they came in. But I couldn't wait to close the door as quickly as possible. As soon as he turned around to leave, I would quickly close the door. It broke my heart every single time. Seeing him walk down the driveway, get into his car and drive off was the worst part. I felt as though he was leaving me all over again – again, and again, and again.

My oldest daughter would go upstairs to her bedroom, sit on her bed looking out of the window, crying. She did this for many weeks. I have no idea if, as he got into his car, he ever saw her sitting on her bedroom window-sill, crying. It was so hard on everyone but especially on her. She found it extremely difficult.

Nothing seemed right. I didn't want to invite him in. In fact, I didn't want him to even 'step inside' the front door. I didn't want him to talk to me – yet it hurt so much when he didn't.

I was a mixture of emotions. Once or twice, I slammed the phone down on him because he had upset me so much. This was not 'us'. This was not our family.

It wasn't the best for the children to witness. That made me feel utterly guilty. So after the first few weeks, my husband and I spoke about it on the phone. We both agreed that the situation was not helpful to the children. We made a commitment to one another that we would try our best not to argue in front of them. Although it has not always been easy to keep to it, we have succeeded. This has been very rewarding for everyone.

Hebrews 12:14-15
(14) Make every effort to live in peace with all men and to be holy; without holiness no-one will see the Lord, (15) See to it that no-one misses the grace of God and that no bitter root grows up to cause trouble and defile many.

James 3:4-8
(4) Or take ships as an example. Although they are so large and are driven by strong winds, they are steered by a very small rudder wherever the pilot wants to go. (5) Likewise the tongue is a small part of the body, but it makes great boasts. Consider what a great forest is set on fire by a small spark. (6) The tongue also is a fire, a world of evil among the parts of the body. It corrupts the whole person, sets the whole course of his life on fire, and is itself set on fire by hell. (7) All kinds of animals, birds, reptiles and creatures of the sea are being tamed and have been tamed by man, (8) but no man can tame the tongue. It is a restless evil, full of deadly poison.

It was really challenging for me to control my words and my emotions. But I knew that I had to. I had to change my attitude and be the peacemaker in my home. It broke my heart to see my children become upset by everything that was happening around them. I am their Mum, their role-model. They look up to me.

I asked God to help me to be calm, loving, and to smile when answering the front door. It was tough. Sometimes it still is. But I made a conscious decision to do it God's way on the doorstep; to show love and gentleness to the man who had caused me so much pain.

I remember struggling with this so much on one particular day. I was visiting one of my very good friends.

Sitting on the couch in her lounge, her cat curled up next to me, I started to share how difficult I was finding the whole 'doorstep experience'.

She looked at me straight in the eye in disbelief and said, "Well! You say that you've forgiven him?" She was waving her arms in the air.

"But I *have*!" I protested. "I *have* forgiven him."

"Well, I'm not sure," she said, shaking her head.

"But I *have* forgiven him *really*," I replied, sinking into the sofa. I was taken aback. She didn't believe me.

"Well." As always, she had gone straight to the heart of the matter. "Surprise him with the unexpected! Invite him in for a cup of tea now and again," she said dismissively.

I looked at her with my eyebrows raised. *Invite him in for a cup of tea! Had she gone mad?* Just *looking* at him was extremely difficult. I wanted to *cry* whenever I *laid eyes* on him. Now my friend was saying that *I should invite him in for a cup of tea!*

My mind was racing with horror. *I couldn't do it! It would be too difficult! How could I make small talk with him!* All I wanted to do was hug him and scream at him at the same time. But he didn't want to hug me, or be screamed at. He didn't want to talk to me at all.

When I looked at him, all I wanted was for him to come home.

I was speechless. She looked down at me, waiting for my reply.

Then she said something to me that I will never forget. She looked directly at me, shook her head and said, "I'm not so sure you've forgiven him."

"Oh no, I *have*," I replied quickly.

"If you've forgiven him, then you need to *show* it!"

I sat there stunned. I didn't like what I was hearing and I didn't want to do it either.

Nothing much more was said after that. I was close to tears but I knew she was right. I believed in my heart that I *had* forgiven him. But what was I *doing* about it? *After what he had done, why should I invite him in for a cup of tea?* The more I thought about it over the next few days, the more I disliked what she had said, especially the part where she thought I had not forgiven him. That really troubled me. I had forgiven him. I was sure of it. I had prayed so much about it. Surely I had forgiven him?

So I decided that I would take her advice and try it.

It was so hard. Even considering it was hard. It made me feel vulnerable and nervous. The doorstep was my most difficult situation. I didn't want him to step into the porch, let alone come into the house. He was not welcome. He had left. He had moved all his stuff out. This was mine and the children's house now. And all this was *his* fault.

A few weeks later I plucked up the courage to invite him in for a cup of tea. Even just asking him made me feel incredibly nervous. *What if he said no? What then? What if he thought I was a complete idiot?* It was excruciating.

He looked at me. He was clearly surprised. He even hesitated. But he accepted the invitation and he stepped into the porch and sat in the lounge. I made him a cup of tea. The children chatted endlessly to him, which was a relief. It took the pressure off me. He only stayed for about half an hour, but it was enough. It was a start.

Since then I have made a deliberate effort to invite him in for a cup of tea. Sometimes he comes in and sometimes he doesn't. I noticed after a few months the tension that I had felt had eased. It became easier to smile, to chat and to be polite. Slowly, things started to change in me too. I began to feel less anxious when the time was drawing nearer for him to arrive. At the sound of him knocking on the front door, I became less panicky and less on edge. The knot in my stomach began to disappear. Instead of feeling overwhelmed with worry, I began to feel less bothered by him arriving. I began to feel as if I could breathe again. I felt a lightness return to my heart and my spirit.

It was the beginning of healing for me in this area.

My friend was right. I had been too caught up in the fear of 'the doorstep'.

So, following this, there have been times when we've invited him in for a cup of tea. That has been OK, but a little awkward at times. The conversation has been polite. The children have taken centre stage which has made it easier.

The children are my priority. I want them to grow up as unaffected as possible by the situation we are facing. I want them to feel peace in their hearts. I don't want them to feel on edge whenever they are around us together. I want them to look back and see that we did our very best for them despite the situation; that we love them and that they are the most important people in our lives.

This has brought my husband and me to a place of being amicable with one another. It has had major advantages.

Being able to talk to one another without shouting and getting angry has given us opportunity to speak about important issues calmly and constructively.

It has enabled us to be flexible with the childcare arrangements. I have invited him to all the necessary school visits, and we have attended as a family.

When situations have arisen which are to do with the children's education, we have approached them together.

God has really helped me to cope with 'the doorstep'. Now it doesn't seem such a barrier. It doesn't grip me with fear or anxiety. I now confidently open the door with a real smile on my face. We may exchange a few words about things, but it is as genuine as it possibly can be.

When my husband walked out of the house, I felt out of control of my life, my marriage and my future.

We are all experiencing the fruitfulness of being amicable. The benefit to our family has been enormously refreshing. There is no animosity flowing over the threshold, no bitterness, hatred, shouting or upset.

Instead, peace and love is flourishing in our home.

I have overcome the battle of 'the doorstep'.

Chapter 10: Forgiveness

The Key to Freedom

> *Colossians 3:12-15*
> *(12) Therefore, as God's chosen people, holy and dearly loved, clothe yourselves with compassion, kindness, humility, gentleness and patience. (13) Bear with each other and forgive whatever grievances you may have against one another. Forgive as the Lord forgave you. (14) And over all these virtues put on love, which binds them all together in perfect unity. (15) Let the peace of Christ rule in your hearts, since as members of one body you were called to peace. And be thankful.*

GOD CALLS US TO FORGIVE

God calls us to forgive those who have hurt us, offended us, rejected us, abandoned us and left us. There is no exception.

It didn't matter how dreadfully my husband had treated me; I knew that God was a God of forgiveness and I needed to forgive my husband.

It is impossible to be completely loving if you are harbouring un-forgiveness in your heart.

My Husband's Birthday

Two days after my husband left, it was his birthday. I woke up with no husband. There was no opening of presents with the children in the morning; there were no kids jumping on the bed, excited that Dad was going to open their presents – nothing! All was quiet in the house. It was just another day.

I felt so sad and lonely. I wondered what he was doing, but only briefly. He was probably with his 'new' woman. He wasn't here and we weren't important. Everything seemed flat and void of excitement: No Dad, no presents, no birthday breakfast in bed. It didn't feel like a normal birthday morning.

It felt so strange. Then I remembered what I was facing that evening. The previous week, when we had been filling in our individual calendars, the subject of his birthday had arisen. For whatever reason, we had decided that we would all go out together to keep things normal for the children.

I didn't want to go, but I felt I had no choice. The children too were desperate for me to go.

I was torn emotionally: I didn't want to go, yet I *did* want to go. I didn't want to see him, yet I *did* want to see him. It was so very difficult. I didn't know what

I was going to say, or how I was going to act. How was I going to get through an entire evening with my husband on his birthday?

Most people would have run a mile and refused to go out to dinner with the man that had just destroyed their marriage and left the family home two days before! I thought that I must have been completely mad! No-one could understand why, but it felt right at the time.

I don't know what I expected. I kept asking myself: *Why does he want me to go with them anyway?* It was all so strange. I was so confused by everything. The children wanted me to go with them. I felt as though I had to.

But there I found myself driving to the bowling alley with the children in the car – all very excited. I felt as if I was wading through sticky mud. I was not prepared for how I would feel when I got there. It took every ounce of effort I could muster to walk through that door and smile.

It didn't feel much like a celebration to me. I tried to look as if I was having fun but I felt extremely uncomfortable.

Questions were going around my head – *Why was I here? What was I doing? Where was 'she', the girlfriend? What had he done this morning? How had he found it all? Was he missing us? Was he missing me?* It felt like emotional torture. I kept talking to the children, clapping at their bowling scores, speaking to them and encouraging them. I didn't want there to be any silences.

I think my bowling score was pretty good. That at least was a bonus! We all had dinner together. There was much chatting and laughing. The children had a great time. I tried my best, but I wasn't myself on the inside. Inside, I was a wreck.

I wanted to scream at him – *Please come home! What are you doing? We miss you!* But I didn't. I sat opposite the man I had loved for so many years and my heart was broken. I tried to appear happy and smiley.

Afterwards, we went back to his flat to give him his presents. That was the worst part for me. First, there had been the dilemma about 'the present'. It had all seemed so confusing and I hadn't known what to do. *Should I purchase him a present? Should I not? If I do, how will that look? If I don't, will that be worse?*

So I had decided to spend only a small amount of money on him. The presents would be 'from the children', even though it was I who had bought them. That felt difficult and awkward. I had purchased a cheap toaster for his flat and had wrapped it up with a few other little things.

I'd had to decide what card to buy. I had no idea that these decisions could be so difficult. Standing there in the shop, all I could see were cards saying 'To my darling husband', 'To the man I love ...' I stood there for many minutes just staring at them. Tears filled my eyes. I struggled to control myself and not to let a tear fall. I turned my eyes away to the next section, but I was surrounded by them. They were everywhere: big, bright, red love-heart ones: 'I love you' ones, teddy bears and 'The Best Husband' ones. They seemed to jump out at me even when I was trying my best to avoid them. It was utterly heartbreaking. I wanted to run out of the shop – fast!

I tried to look for three cards from the children. I was scanning the titles and all of them seemed to be just as bad. All I could see was 'To the Best Dad in the World.' I stood there thinking, *I can't buy that either from the children. He isn't the best Dad in the world! He had just left them! He isn't the best husband either.*

Who would have thought that standing in a card aisle could be so overwhelming, so claustrophobic, so daunting, *so* painful? I deliberately chose cards with no words in them at all.

Then, what to write? As I stood with pen in hand at the kitchen table, all I could think was – *What do I write?* Do I say '*love* from?' or not? Do I put a kiss at the end, or not? I didn't want to write anything. In fact, if I hadn't been going to the 'party', I wouldn't have given him a card at all! Then I wouldn't have had to make all these painful decisions … or write in the card!

It had all been so stressful. I knew that I ought to give him a card because I was seeing him in person. So there I sat – in *his* flat. He had absolutely no idea of the ordeal I had faced in buying those presents and those cards.

I felt out of place. I didn't jump up and offer to make the cups of tea. I didn't know what to do. I just sat there, being very quiet!

As I looked around, I could see all his things dotted about. He had moved in. It felt so strange, so surreal. All the stuff that I had lived with and had walked past on a daily basis was sitting here on shelves as though it all belonged there. I felt as if *I* was an ornament, perching uncomfortably on the edge of the sofa.

I didn't like it! I didn't like it at all! I began to feel really out of place and on edge. I tried hard to keep my composure, smiling and nodding where appropriate and making conversation in places. At the same time, I could feel myself becoming more and more alert. Trying to appear casual, I kept looking around for any signs of 'the other woman's things'. I was so relieved that I saw none. I kept thinking – '*What will I do if I do see 'her' stuff?*' I'm not really sure what I would have done if I had.

I didn't like being there! It was a lovely flat but I was so aware that 'she' would have been there. I couldn't wait to leave. It wasn't our home; he wasn't on vacation. This was *his* home now. *How did I sit there?* I don't know. But I did.

The children presented him with his presents. They seemed happy to give them to him. He opened them graciously, making a huge fuss of them, thanking the children and hugging them. He also thanked me for the toaster.

Unexpectedly, I felt an overwhelming wave of guilt! In fact, as I looked at the small cluster of tiny presents I felt so very *mean.* They really were hardly anything at all. The way he gushed over how wonderful they were made me squirm in my seat! I felt really embarrassed! It didn't seem enough. I was unprepared for the feeling of guilt. Isn't that bizarre?

As he opened each present, he smiled and made such a fuss that it made me feel even worse. The only reason I had bought him those few presents was because the children were so used to giving him a few each to open.

Normally we spoiled each other on our birthdays. There had always been many presents to open. We used to make a list for each other of what we wanted and we loved buying each other gifts and would spoil each other rotten. Our thinking would be that we spent so much on the children all year that we deserved a treat too. Not this time. This time it was not the same, not the same at all.

The children wedged the candles into the cake I had bought him and we all sang *Happy Birthday*. He blew out the candles. I was relieved that I had gone to the effort of buying the birthday cake *as well*. I felt as though I had made the whole thing bearable. I was very aware that if the children hadn't had anything to give their Dad to open on his birthday, they themselves would have felt awkward and upset.

We all had a slice of cake. The children seemed to enjoy it – and it appeared like an adventure for them – *Dad's new place*. This was the first time they had seen it.

When we left, I got in the car and I sighed with relief. I never wanted to go back there again. Just being there made me feel so unloved.

When we got home and the children were all tucked up, I sat on my bed and prayed. I desperately needed God to help me get through this. I cried.

It had felt right to go out with the family for his birthday, even if it *was* only two days after he had left us. I had forgiven him as best as I could. I praise God that I was able to do that before he had left. I believed with all of my heart that somewhere in all this mess I was doing the right thing.

I cried so many tears into my pillow. The evening had reinforced everything – he didn't love me, not one bit.

A few days later I wrote in my diary:

> Yesterday I felt really unhappy and sad all day. I realised that 'my' agenda is not my husband's. I have to let him go. I have to move forward or I'll become stuck – bitter and angry. It will eat me up!
>
> So today, I've decided to ask God to be with my husband on his journey. God's timing is perfect. God can't use me effectively if I am walking with a heart of bitterness and anger. But God can use me if I'm walking with a heart of love.
>
> The hardest part is that (as his wife) I have no say over anything my husband does. We are no longer a couple. We no longer talk about things together. I just need to trust God and not to doubt.

> I need to change my focus from what I want my husband 'to do' – to what God wants 'me' to do?
>
> I believe that God is going to do mighty things. God is powerful, majestic and awesome!

Holding onto un-forgiveness is a sin. God knows our hearts. He sees everything. He sees our actions, hears our words, knows our thoughts and our intentions. God knows if there is anything we are hiding.

Un-forgiveness is ugly. It rips apart families and friends. It destroys the soul, slowly eating away at a person like a deadly disease. It is incredibly consuming.

It robs a person of joy, hope, peace and clarity. It seeps into one's mind and seems to saturate everything in hatred, anger, bitterness and negativity. *What is the point of that?*

I did not want any part of that ugliness. I wanted freedom. I wanted to walk in love.

But it was one of the hardest, most difficult emotional challenges I had ever had to deal with. I had made a conscious and very real decision to forgive my husband that day as we sat at the coffee table. What I didn't anticipate was the continuous effort it took on my part. It seemed to me that I had to do all the work.

As I had to see him twice a week regarding child care arrangements, I was in a place of total insecurity. I realised that, although I had forgiven him, I still felt very vulnerable whenever I came into contact with him. I felt hurt and, at times, still angry at the little things. I had to work at forgiving him on a daily basis. It was something I had to work through on my own. All the time I knew that I didn't want to fall into the trap of un-forgiveness. I knew that I could have done that at any stage.

I have met people who have openly said, "I hate my husband for what he has done to me!"

The word 'hate' often seems to be spat out with the full force of anger! It has taken me by surprise and made me step back, almost wince. That is not for me!

I was not going to allow myself to become twisted, bitter or angry. I was not prepared to compromise on my faith and walk in sin.

I knew that, without forgiveness, relationships break down and can be completely destroyed. Families are divided, torn apart and left in ruins. I wanted something different for us.

It is only now that I fully realise that God showed me how very important forgiveness was. It was not for my husband necessarily, but it was for me.

Forgiveness has enabled me to walk in love, confidence and peace. It has given my daily walk purpose and meaning. Most importantly, it has given me the freedom to smile.

I made a conscious decision to try my best to speak kindly towards my husband. There were times when I didn't succeed. My children still hold me to account for this. I once swore angrily at him down the telephone. I used only one swearword but that alone was enough. My children were not used to hearing me use bad language. My youngest promptly burst into tears and screamed, "Mummy, STOP shouting at Daddy!" That made it worse!

True forgiveness has to remain true forgiveness. The rewards of forgiveness are underestimated. Forgiveness brings total healing.

Forgiveness did not replace the devastation I felt. That was still present.

Instead, forgiveness helped me and my children to grow as a new family. Gradually, as the weeks and months went by, we picked up the pieces and started afresh. By just the smallest action, such as speaking kindly about my husband, my children instinctively spoke positively about their Dad.

My Dad once said that my husband's adultery was like a pebble, a pebble that had been dropped into a pool of water, creating a ripple that had affected our entire family.

But I believe that forgiveness also works in the same way. I had to choose what I dropped into that water: I chose forgiveness. It *had* to start with me, even if I didn't realise it at the time. Over the months, our family and friends have also been able to work through their issues.

I have discovered that walking in forgiveness is a daily, personal choice. It has tested me to the core.

About a month after he had moved out of our family home I was praying to God. I was hurting and angry. On this particular day I felt God show me that I had to *love* my husband *beyond* how I felt. That meant doing something out of the ordinary, even though it was the last thing I wanted to do, kind things which I knew would not be expected or appreciated.

This was going to be difficult for me.

A few weeks later I was making dinner. It was his turn to collect the children and look after them at his place. As I was preparing the meal, I decided to make enough for him to take a portion back to his flat.

As I started to put his dinner on a plate, my son walked into the kitchen. I started to wrap the plate in foil. He asked me what I was doing and I explained that I was giving Dad some dinner.

He said, "Mum, why do you make Dad dinner? He doesn't even care about you!"

I replied, "I love Daddy very much, and he may not have time to make it himself tonight." He shook his head in disgust and walked off.

When my husband arrived to collect the children, I handed him the plate of food along with some pudding. He looked at me in surprise and said, "What's that for?"

"I just wanted to bless you," I replied smiling.

He was a little taken aback with a puzzled expression on his face. He broke into a smile and said, "*Bless* me?"

It was probably a little strange, but I was obedient to God. I smiled at him. I didn't expect anything in return either. I wasn't doing this for him, but I did it for God.

As he sheepishly smiled back at me, I felt an incredible peace. What I discovered was that there was no room for anger to grow; only peace. I realised that peace and love were far better than the alternative.

That evening I wrote in my diary:

> None of this would be possible without God constantly nudging me, moulding me, changing my attitude and changing my heart.

Sometime later, I was shopping and I picked up a packet of custard slices. My husband was due to look after the children at my house later that day which was unusual.

When I got home I put a custard slice in the fridge for him. As I was leaving to go to work, I wrote him a card to say that there was a custard slice in the fridge just for him.

After I returned home from work later that day, as he was leaving, he turned around and gave me a big hug.

I wasn't expecting that! In fact, I wasn't expecting anything. Again, I didn't do it for him; I did it for God. The difference was that I did it with a heart of love, a genuine heart of love, still expecting nothing in return.

God has shown me that, when I surrender all to Him, even if I don't like it, He turns all things around for good. Even when I can't see past my own insecurities, God has a plan. God knows the whole situation. He told me to trust Him and I did.

I cooked a simple meal and made enough for one extra portion. It wasn't difficult. God didn't show me to do something that I wasn't capable of doing. Cooking a meal is easy.

That, I find, is one of the most amazing things about God. He asks me to do the very simple things. Yet often, I don't necessarily want to hear it, or do it!

That big hug on the doorstep made me smile; it really did. My husband was blessed and so was I. Reaching out with a heart of love in the most dire circumstances proved to be amazing.

Nothing changed however. He didn't come back; that wasn't the agenda.

I wrote in my diary:

> I don't feel that horrible anger, disappointment or rejection so much now when I look at him, because I have made a decision to be different in my attitude. By being nice and by following God's plan things are so much better!
> Love heals.

> Forgiveness doesn't make excuses or cover over the truth of what he has done. The truth is the truth.
>
> Love enabled me to walk in grace and humility. It has brought gentleness to my heart.

I was becoming aware that I needed to maintain a positive attitude wherever possible.

I realise that in freeing me, it has also freed my children. They are not caught in a vile trap of angry words tossed back and forth between their parents. They are not witness to sarcastic comments or to ugly, angry texts or phone calls. They do not feel frightened, nervous or anxious when I open the front door to their Dad.

Instead, they are free to enjoy their time spent with him. That has been crucial for them. It is only as I look back now that I realise this has been God's best for all of us.

It has also freed our extended family and friends to spend time with my husband without feeling as if they had to 'take sides' or worry about offending me.

Forgiveness is vital for healing – healing of heart and soul. I do not need to carry the *weight* of the pain any longer!

Forgiveness is the key to freedom.

Chapter 11: Love

Love IS Powerful

> *1 Corinthians 13:4-8*
> *(4) Love is patient, love is kind. It does not envy, it does not boast, it is not proud. (5) It is not rude, it is not self-seeking, it is not easily angered, it keeps no record of wrongs. (6) Love does not delight in evil but rejoices with the truth. (7) It always protects, always trusts, always hopes, always perseveres. (8a) Love never fails.*

A few months after my husband moved out, I discovered that he was going on holiday abroad with his mistress. This was not just anywhere abroad, but to her home town where her family lived.

It completely floored me. It was as if the rug had been pulled out beneath me. *Holiday? Abroad?* Was he going to meet her family? *How could he do that?* What about *me?* What about our family?

There I sat, on the floor in my lounge, my legs curled up underneath me, tear drops falling onto my jeans. The pain in my heart was overwhelming. My face was red, blotchy and tear-stained. I couldn't stop crying.

I didn't understand. *How could he leave me? What did I do?*

After a while there was a knock on my front door. Instantly, fear rose up in my heart. I didn't want to answer it. Maybe they would go away. I didn't move. A second knock followed, louder this time. I still didn't move. I looked across the lounge in panic. Everything was a mess. I was embarrassed.

I heard a familiar voice through the letterbox. It was one of my closest friends. She sounded persistent *and* didn't seem to be going away. I had to move.

I glanced at myself in the mirror. I looked dreadful. I looked down at my clothes; even they looked a mess. I felt terrible. Why today?

I walked to the front door. Slowly I opened it, half-peering around it, hoping she wouldn't see me. "Hello," I muttered, hoping she wouldn't notice my tear-stained face. She stood there smiling at me. I had no choice. I couldn't leave her there. I hesitated for a moment, then I opened the door wider. She stepped inside, reached out and flung her arms around me. I was overwhelmed. That was it; I disintegrated.

She had absolutely no idea what was wrong with me. I was mortified that she was seeing me like this. I was a complete and utter wreck. She saw me at my very worst, in the pit of pain.

I was so grateful that my friend had turned up. She was wonderful. She just sat there, listening to me. I was no longer alone; I was no longer unloved. I didn't have to carry the weight of my grief on my own.

I still hadn't given up hope that my husband would return home to me and the children. That is why the pain of him going on holiday with *her* was so bad. It felt as if he had betrayed me yet again. I believed with all my heart that God could do a miracle.

I share this because it demonstrated God's love to me.

She did tell me later that morning that she had had a full schedule planned for that particular day, but because God had prompted her to visit me, she cancelled everything in her diary and drove to my house instead. She trusted God enough to do something out of the ordinary. She didn't phone me first either. She simply knocked on my front door.

That also amazes me about God. I'm unsure if I would have answered the phone. If I had answered the phone, I would have said that I was 'fine', brushed it all aside and pretended everything was going well. Then she probably would not have visited me.

I'm so glad she did. Isn't God amazing!

One day, when I was walking home, I saw a frog lying there on the pavement. I stopped and stared at it. It looked horrible. It was dead. I felt so sorry for the poor little thing; it had dried up in the sun and had not been able to reach water.

As I looked at it, I knew in my heart in that very moment that I did not want to end up like that frog: dried up, useless, dead and lifeless. Those are the very things that happen if we walk away from God. Our hearts turn dry and we become ineffective for God. As I turned my eyes away and walked towards my house, I had such a conviction in my heart. I needed God. I needed to be *drenched* in the Holy Spirit daily.

I wrote in my diary that evening:

> I feel no hatred, anger, malice, resentment, bitterness – only love. I feel confident that God is at the wheel. He is in the driving seat. I may be too small to see where I am going, but God knows exactly where I am going.

Months previously, I was preparing a sermon and God gave me a word:

> Love dispels the darkness.

When we love, there is no room for hate. Love and hate cannot be mixed together.

Baptisms

On the 25th April 2010, two months after my husband had left, our two daughters were being baptised at our church. Baptism is where a person is fully immersed in water in a baptismal pool in front of the members of the church.

I had invited everyone from the church to attend the baptism and to stay for food afterwards. Not only that, but the girls had invited *all* our family and friends, nearly forty in total. Most of them had never been to a Baptist church before and had never witnessed a baptism before either.

I was a little concerned. *What would they all think? Would they think it strange?*

Putting on a party, setting up the church hall, didn't faze me. The baptism and the party was not the problem. My husband was the problem! They had invited him also. He was going to be there. It was a big problem! I was trying to hold myself together.

What would it be like? It felt weird already! *How was I going to look at him? What would I say? What would I do? What would the family say to him? What would the family do? How would everyone react?* It was overwhelming just thinking about it.

On the Friday, two days before the event, I arranged to meet my husband for lunch in town to discuss the baptism. It was the first time we had met on our own since he had moved out.

This was a challenge in itself. I woke up that morning thinking crazy thoughts like: *What do I wear? What will I say? What if it goes horribly wrong?*

I had prayed about that lunch meeting from the moment it was booked in the diary. I was apprehensive. I was quite scared at meeting him for lunch. Not scared of him, but scared about my emotions. *What if I melted into floods of tears? What if he mentioned 'her'? What if he wanted to bring her along?* My mind was racing.

I walked to the coffee shop, getting there ridiculously early. I wanted to be prepared. I ordered myself a cup of tea and glanced around at the seating plan. It seemed difficult to choose the 'right' seat.

I sat down on a stool by the window. I took out my book that I had packed in my bag earlier. I said thank you to the lady as she presented me with my cup of tea. I sat there for a few minutes looking out of the window. I wanted to appear relaxed. I didn't want him to walk in and me be on tenterhooks. I had half an hour to spare.

I opened my handbag and took out my foundation palette. I looked at myself in the mirror, touched up my make-up and readjusted my hair. I sighed. I opened my book. I looked down at the first page. Then I looked again out of the window. I checked my watch. *Twenty minutes to go.* OK! I'm calm. *Breathe!*

I tried to read the first line but I couldn't concentrate on a single word. It was a silly idea to bring a book. I closed the front cover. I took a sip of my tea. I couldn't drink that either.

I checked my mobile phone for any messages, just in case he had cancelled. *No.* No messages. *Fifteen minutes to go.*

I reached across to the left-hand side of the window-sill and picked up an old book. It was a recipe book. That seemed easier reading; only little sentences to digest, and pictures. That was better. I randomly opened it and tried my best to find the contents interesting. I glanced again at my watch. *Ten minutes to go.*

I picked up my cup. I was surprised I didn't drop it into my lap. I was so nervous!

Slowly I sipped my tea, trying to make it last as long as possible, desperately trying to appear casual. I didn't want to rush it and sit alone with nothing to drink. Picking up the teacup helped my nerves.

I immersed myself in the page of the recipe book. It was all about different chicken recipes. Time went by. A bell sounded. The door swung open.

I glanced up. There he was, my husband. He walked around the door and smiled at me.

In that very moment I felt so glad that I had arrived early. I felt composed, calm and ready.

I smiled back. "Hi!" I said, hoping I appeared casual and confident, although just looking at him brought a swarm of butterflies to my stomach. I tried not to appear nervous.

"Hi!" he said back, still smiling. He perched himself on the stool next to me and slung his jacket to one side.

As I looked at him, I saw the man I loved, the man who had left me, the man who had moved out six weeks prior.

He didn't look nervous.

We ordered sandwiches, coffee and tea. When we started to speak, it felt quite awkward, but we both smiled and spoke in a kind manner to each other. It was not a frosty atmosphere. There were no silences in the conversation, no looking at the floor.

We kept the conversation to the plans for the baptism. Then he said something that stunned me. I asked him where he was going to sit on Sunday.

"Next to you, if that's OK?" he said.

I was a little taken aback. That was not expected.

"Really? Next to me? Why?" I said, flabbergasted.

"Well, you're the only one who will talk to me," he said with a slight chuckle in his voice. He rapidly looked down at his plate.

I sat there and looked at him. What an incredible statement! Out of all the people he could have asked, *he's asking me?*

I chuckled; so did he again.

"OK," I said, secretly very relieved. It was the part I had been dreading the most. Where would he sit? If he sat at the back or we sat separately, then people in the church would wonder why. Only a few people from church knew that we had separated. I didn't want there to be questions, but I had no idea what his thoughts were on the matter.

"OK," I replied, "that would be really good. I will save you a seat next to me," I said, smiling.

On the Sunday, as the service was about to start, we took our seats. Our family and friends took up four rows. We all sat on one side together. My husband had arrived, and we sat together as arranged. It did feel strange but at the same time it gave me security.

During the baptism, everyone was invited to crowd around the baptismal pool at the front of the church. As my daughters stepped into the pool one at a time, I felt so very proud of them. I felt so very privileged and honoured to have been asked to baptise them.

As I stood there in the water, I looked up in awe. All I could see were the faces of our friends and family. Each of them was there, smiling.

I am sure it was difficult for some of them to see my husband there. But all the family spoke to him. The day was a huge success. It was a huge testimony to God that He had brought us all together at the most difficult of times.

With God's love and mercy, our two families, which had been torn apart, found themselves greeting one another, mingling and laughing.

I believe that was the start of the healing for our families.

When we got home, I was absolutely exhausted. It was one of the most difficult things I had done so far, but I had done it. I had walked in love.

On the following Friday, one of the children's leaders at church took me to one side. She said something which spoke volumes to me.

She said, "I didn't know what to do when I saw your husband at the baptism. I didn't know whether to go up to him or not. But then I thought, if Toni, as his wife, can talk to him and hug him, *so can I*. So I went up to him and said, "Hi!"

I wrote in my diary that evening:

> I never realised the impact that all this has had on other people. But she saw me loving my husband regardless of the pain and agony he had caused me. It caused her to have the same compassion towards him and to act in love. How awesome!

I never really realised that people were watching me to see how I behaved towards him. I had never given it a thought.

I'm so very glad that she was able to go up to my husband without any fear of 'hurting me' by doing so. She was able to approach him with a heart of love and sincerity, rather than avoiding him.

Love dismantles the strongest of walls. Love heals, transforms and forgives. Love radiates.

Love: such a small word; such an enormous word.

Love *is* powerful.

Chapter 12: Letting Go

Needing an Answer

I made a decision in July 2010.

I decided that I would keep praying for our marriage until our wedding anniversary in November. If nothing had changed after that date, I would let it go. If my husband had not come back by then, I would stop praying for our marriage.

I had such incredible faith and hope that God would work a miracle and would save our marriage.

I had invested nearly twenty years of my life in loving my husband. I couldn't give up on my marriage just like that.

I had to set myself a date.

There were no signs that we were going to get back together. But I had hope. I still loved him.

October 2010

The month before our anniversary I asked my husband if we could meet for dinner. He agreed. I bought a new dress and made an extra effort to look nice. I wanted to ask him what he wanted. *Where did he see his future? Our future? Did he want to come back or not? Did he want a divorce?* I had a list of big questions and I *needed* answers, I *wanted* answers. I wanted him to come home to me. I wanted him to say that he was really sorry and that he had made a big mistake! I wanted him to leave this woman and come back … to say that he loved me and that he missed me.

'Not knowing' was so incredibly frustrating. I didn't know what he was thinking so I wanted to discuss things clearly.

As the evening approached, I began to feel quite on edge, and very nervous. *What was going to happen?*

We met for dinner and I asked all the questions I wanted to ask. He answered them. Some answers were very hard for me to hear. Some made me upset, but I needed to hear them. I needed answers.

He told me that he had "never thought about coming back, not once". That hurt. That hurt a lot.

"Do you want a divorce then?" I asked him, trying to look him straight in the eye. He was fidgeting and squirming on the other side of the table.

"Yes," he said quietly, his eyes staring at the table.

I felt shocked. This wasn't going to plan. There was nowhere else to go. No other options. What was left?

I sat there stunned for a while, thinking about what he had said. I wanted to keep my composure. I didn't want to react with tears either.

So I replied simply, "Yes, I want a divorce too."

I was not going to beg or plead with him to change his mind. I knew then and there that he was not going to change. His mind was made up. So was mine.

November 2010

A few weeks went past and our 18th wedding anniversary arrived. It was a sad day for me.

It felt as if I had been carrying an overwhelmingly urgent weight of prayer for my husband for a very long time.

I had prayed for him ever since I became a Christian. But this was different. This had been an intense daily battle of prayer for him for the last nine months, for our marriage, our family, our children, and for our future.

Letting go was an important step for me.

I wrote in my diary:

> Just because God has not worked a miracle today, I am not going to give up on God! I am not going to give up believing in God! I'm not going to stop praying!
>
> Just because I have not got my way today – who knows what God has in store? I believe it must be something good – something I cannot see – something awesome – something that brings glory to God.

Monday 29th November 2010

As I sat in bed, I was praying to God. The sun started to shine through the curtains, creating a silhouette of my pot plant behind the curtains on the window-sill. It looked like a dove with outstretched wings, ready to take flight. The shape was so clear. The dove's head and beak looked beautiful.

As I looked at it, I felt God saying to me:

> OK, this is a new day – a new start – you are ready to fly solo. Your wings have been clipped for long enough – now it's time to fly. It's OK.

A few days later, I came to a place where I could take my rings off my finger.

It was very emotional for me. I sat on my bed and cried when I put them in a little box. They meant a great deal to me. They reminded me of our wedding day, of the commitment we had made to each other, of the love we had once had for each other.

I didn't realise the attachment I had to the rings until I had to take them off. But I knew it was the right thing to do. I couldn't look at them on my finger for another day.

I wandered around the house, taking down all our wedding pictures. This made me cry even more. They were beautiful.

I found the courage shortly afterwards to pick up the phone and make an appointment to see a solicitor about getting a divorce.

During the phone call I was advised that, on my first visit, I needed to hand in our marriage certificate. I asked the receptionist, "Do you take a copy and give it back to me?"

"No," she said, "we keep it and it goes to the Court."

"Oh," I replied, quite taken aback. "How long for?" I asked.

"You don't get it back," she replied. "The Court keeps it."

"Oh, OK," I replied. I was not expecting that. I didn't even know how important my marriage certificate was until that moment. I put the phone down and walked upstairs. I felt overwhelmed. I found it, and as I picked it up, tears pricked my eyes. .

This was it: no going back; the end.

I held it in my hands. It made me smile. My signature looked so different. We had married so young. I closed my eyes and put my hands on it and prayed. I said "Lord, let Your will be done."

As I prayed, the tears rolled down my face. I went downstairs and I scanned a copy before I put it into the envelope, knowing it would be the last time I would ever see it. I found it really difficult. I sealed the envelope quickly and left the house. I locked the front door and drove to the solicitor's premises. I parked the car and opened the door of the office. I tried not to cry.

After handing the envelope over to the receptionist, I left the office building, closing the door behind me. I stepped straight into a fresh, icy wind. As I crossed the road and opened my car, I thought to myself, "Well, that's it!"

I was still standing. I just needed to take one day at a time.

I needed to let go of the old and step into the new.

Chapter 13: The Value of Family

Unity

December 2010

It was my birthday in a few days and I felt so lonely. I carried a heaviness of grief in my heart. I felt like crying. It was going to be my first birthday without my husband. Without us being a family unit. Everything felt different and I wasn't looking forward to it.

On this particular day, the children and I had been invited to my neighbour's house for a birthday roast dinner. I wanted to go, but at the same time, I didn't. I could have chosen instead to have an early night, keeping the world at bay. My emotions were all over the place.

I was trying so hard to move on and now this small fact of my birthday felt as if I had run head-first into a brick wall. I was on the brink of crying when I arrived at my hairdresser's that morning.

She was also one of my best friends. She knew me very well. We had prayed together many times and had spent much time together with our families over the years.

I walked through the door and sat on her couch. I can't remember what she said to me, but something about my birthday coming up. I burst into tears. Not just a few tears either.

I really did feel sorry for myself. Normally I would have been excited about my birthday, but not this year. Especially since our anniversary was only a few weeks away.

I wanted to hide from all of it, watching television and wrapped in a blanket.

My very good friend made me a cup of tea and passed me tissues. Eventually I stopped crying and calmed down. We got up and moved into her salon. It had been a while since my last haircut. As I looked at myself in the mirror, I decided to have my long hair cut off. I needed not only to 'be' a new person, but to 'look like' a new person. So she cut my hair into a chin-length bob. It looked great. It made me feel better too!

Then she went into the kitchen and came up to me holding a birthday cake, singing *Happy Birthday*. Wow! That really did cheer me up!

I told her that I was going out later that evening to my neighbour's house for a roast dinner. She smiled at me, handing me flowers and a birthday card. It was so unexpected.

Later that evening, as I was nearly ready, the phone rang. It was my neighbour. I checked my watch. I wasn't late. For once! I had ten more minutes before I would be on time.

"Where are you?" she said.

"I'm just getting ready," I replied.

"Well, can you hurry up? Dinner is on the table!" she said.

"But I'm not even late yet!" I replied laughing. "OK, we'll be there in a few minutes."

I ran downstairs and was about to put on my green wellington boots. It had been snowing days earlier, leaving sleet and a slippery glass-like surface. I stopped and checked my reflection in the mirror.

I had bought my sparkly gold dress a few weeks earlier after I had been instructed to wear something 'posh'.

I decided against the green wellington boots and opted for my furry brown boots.

We all put on our coats. It was freezing outside. As we walked the few steps to my neighbour's, we had to cling onto the outside walls for support. As we walked carefully up her driveway, her front door opened and she ushered us inside.

I walked into her lounge and opened the double doors into the kitchen – "SURPRISE!" everyone shouted! I stood there in amazement, covered in streamers. All my family and friends were there – in my neighbour's kitchen! I broke into a very big smile and went very red. I was utterly speechless!

There was my Mum, Dad, Nan and my mother-in-law. My family and friends from church, including my friend whom I had seen that morning. It turned out that she had known about the party all along. I couldn't believe it.

My Mum and my neighbour had been organising this surprise birthday party for me for months! I had no clue! I didn't suspect a thing. Everyone had even been told to park their cars in different streets!

There was an overflowing abundance of love in that room.

I felt so loved in that single moment. As I write this, tears have welled up in my eyes. It touched my heart so deeply. It meant so much to me, that my family and friends would organise something so special for me. They had known that I would find my birthday difficult.

But what I had been dreading turned into something so very beautiful. It was such a lovely surprise. It was stunning! I couldn't stop smiling.

That evening something shifted in my heart.

As I looked into the faces of the people that I loved, I had an overwhelming sense that everything was going to work out. I was going to get through this heartache. I realised that I had this wonderful support network surrounding me.

I couldn't stop smiling all evening. When I climbed into bed that evening, I could hardly sleep because I was still smiling. Even in the morning, as I woke up, I still felt on top of the world.

Easter 2011
I had booked myself into a ladies' conference with a couple of friends. I was unsure what to do about the house. The children could stay with their Dad but I didn't want to leave the house unoccupied for five days. We had a cat that was quite elderly and I didn't like the idea of leaving her for too long.

So I made a decision to ask my husband if he would stay at my house with our children for that time while I would be away. I knew that the children would be happier remaining at home amongst their things and surrounded by their friends. I liked the idea of the children and the cat being looked after.

He agreed. I was a little surprised that he was prepared to stay at my house, as it must have seemed a little odd.

I prayed about it and I felt in my heart that God was showing me that I had to see it as a blessing.

I did my best to leave everything in order and make everything seem stress-free for them. The freezer was stocked and the house was tidy. I set off for the conference with love in my heart and peace in my spirit. I was excited to see what God had in store for me in those few days.

I had a great time. Five days later, exhausted but smiling, I knocked on my front door. I walked into an atmosphere of family: there they all were, relaxing in the lounge, watching a film together. I was greeted with hugs and kisses from the children.

Then they all sat as if it were Christmas morning. They were so excited. They knew that I would have brought them home a small gift or two. As was our tradition, I handed them all a little something. The last one I gave to my husband. He was surprised.

I remember taking ages in the gift shop on the last day of the conference. I couldn't give him nothing; that would have been mean. So, after much deliberating, I had settled on an old-fashioned Union Jack tin. I really liked it. I thought he could put it on his desk.

I felt sheepish as I handed him his present. It wasn't necessary that I had bought him a gift but it was nice. He seemed to like it.

The children disappeared into the kitchen and emerged moments later, my youngest daughter holding a 'welcome home' cake that she had made. It was a wonderful surprise.

A year ago I found it difficult to speak to my husband on the doorstep; let alone invite him in for a cup of tea. I had really wanted to go to that conference and I didn't want to leave the house empty.

When I came back and saw everyone relaxing and enjoying themselves, it struck me how beautiful it was to see unity within our home, even if we were never going back to the way things were.

Summer 2011

In the summer I received an invitation in the post to attend my nephew's dedication at a church which was three hours' drive away. My nephew is my husband's brother's little boy.

As the date got nearer, my husband asked how we were travelling there. I was driving, yet I was sure I would get lost on the way. So we decided that we would all go together in my car: the children, my husband and me.

As we got nearer to the church, we stopped for coffee. It seemed strange to walk into the café together and sit down, drinking tea and eating cakes. It felt like old times. We sat by the window on big oversized seats. The sun shone through the glass and we passed the time making conversation and laughing together.

When we arrived at the church, it did feel a little strange that we were arriving together, but it didn't seem to faze the rest of the family. There was much greeting and hugging when we walked through the door.

Then the most unexpected thing happened. My sister-in-law pulled me to one side and asked me if I would like to be godmother to her son, my nephew! Wow! *Me!* I was so overwhelmed with joy. It was such a privilege and honour to be asked.

Even though I was getting divorced from my husband, my brother-in-law and his family were saying that they wanted me to be part of their lives for ever. I was taken aback! I couldn't stop smiling.

During the service, I sat next to my husband, our children, and my husband's family. We all had a lovely time. It was great to see my children running around with their cousins, surrounded by their grandparents, aunties and uncles.

As I drove home, we chatted and laughed all the way. There was no tension. I'm sure there could have been, but there was no need for there to be any. We had all enjoyed spending our day together with the wider family.

Family

During the week of '7 Days of Agony' (Chapter 5), I was sitting in the chair in the lounge. My husband hadn't made any decision at that stage. Fear and a deep agonising sadness gripped my heart. Tears raced down my cheeks.

The fear of separation raised so many questions. All I could think about at that time was: *What about my mother-in-law, my brothers-in-law, their families, my nieces and nephews? What about them?* How would this affect them? Thoughts circled around my head.

Would they ever want to see me again? Tears tumbled in big blobs into the awaiting tissues. I loved my *family* so much. I sat and cried even more.

I am an only child. I had always wanted brothers and sisters. When I married my husband, he had three brothers and a close family friend who was like another brother. He also had a sister-in-law. They became *my* brothers-in-law and sister-in-law. When we said the words "I do", his family accepted me into their family. They became my family. I became part of his family just as he became part of mine.

Now here I found myself twenty years later thinking of what it would mean to me to lose them. I needn't have been anxious.

Reaching Out

I have always enjoyed trying out new recipes, cooking for our family and entertaining. I didn't realise until my husband moved out how much I had enjoyed cooking for the five of us. It took me weeks to get used to setting the table for four. I missed so many things about mealtimes.

It became very difficult sitting at the table with the children. They were hurting too and didn't always want to say much.

They missed their Dad terribly. He had always been the fun one. He was the one who made them laugh at the table. We used to spend ages sitting at the table eating dinner and chatting about our days.

Since my husband had moved out it didn't seem as much fun as it used to be. I would ask them about their day but they wouldn't say very much. It became a chore.

I thought that it was time that we started entertaining again.

But it was rather daunting. So I made a decision. I was going to battle my fears! We were going to invite people over regardless.

I sat down with the children in the first few weeks and I asked them if they would like us to invite people to dinner. They thought it was a great idea, so we made a list. The children were quite excited about the prospect. On the other hand, I was apprehensive. We had always had our friends and family over for dinner regularly. But this was different. We wanted to invite people from church who had been a great help to us. Just putting pen to paper made me realise that I had no confidence at all.

The next Sunday I approached one of the youth leaders. I was extremely nervous but I asked her and her husband if they would like to come to our house for dinner. They agreed and we put a date in the diary. It went surprisingly well.

That was the beginning. Since then, our house has been full of people. My youngest daughter enjoys baking. She has baked many chocolate cakes, cupcakes and pancakes.

Entertaining our family and friends has changed the atmosphere in our house to one of laughter and joy.

I have discovered that I can do it.

I don't have the support of that second person, but the children and I are a new family. We have enjoyed it immensely. It has proved to be such an incredible blessing. Out of this journey we have made many new friends.

It was not easy. I had to step out of the boat and out of my comfort zone into the unknown just at the time when my confidence had been battered. I felt scared that people would think I was boring. I'm so glad that I didn't let those fears stop me.

What a transformation! We now enjoy having people over to our house. I don't worry so much about tidying every nook and cranny first either. People have to walk in and take us as they find us. It takes a brave person to reach out a hand of friendship and invite people to their house for a cup of tea and a slice of cake. But it is worth the effort.

Christmas Day 2011

I was woken up fairly early on Christmas Day morning. One by one the children each piled into my bedroom holding their Christmas stockings.

Like last year, I also took mine off my door handle and we sat together opening our presents. It was so much fun. Afterwards we went downstairs and opened presents from each other.

It was so relaxing and enjoyable. The day before was Christmas Eve and I had set the table for Christmas Day. It looked beautiful. I had made an extra effort this year, because we had invited a guest to join us for Christmas lunch. That *guest* was my ex-husband.

When I realised he didn't have plans for Christmas Day a few weeks prior, I decided to ask him to join us. I had purchased new table mats, table cloths and accessories. I had chosen a red and gold theme. Crackers were laid out, serviettes fanned into glasses, sparkly sprinkles covered the table and candles were the centrepiece.

The vegetables were all peeled and ready in the saucepans waiting to be cooked. The turkey and vegetarian nut roast had been cooked already. Everything I could prepare in advance was done.

I had also struggled to know what to do regarding present-buying. *Should I buy my ex-husband a present? What if I don't? What if I do?* So I decided to ignore all my questions and buy him a few presents.

I knew that I would feel terrible if he joined us for Christmas Day and I didn't give him presents to open. The children would give him a few, but it didn't feel right not to give him presents. So I did buy extra presents for him. I wanted him to feel loved. I wanted him to enjoy the day too.

I wanted the day to be enjoyable for everyone.

The time went so quickly. He was only with us until 3.30pm. The children had such a good day. They really like having him there together.

I was looking forward to the day, even if it seemed a little out of the ordinary to have my ex-husband joining us for lunch. It was a good decision to invite him. I'm glad that I did. I have no idea what next Christmas will be like. I have decided that traditions are great, but we are also open to change.

I don't know what my ex-husband thought about it. How he felt. He said that he had had a nice time. I hope that he felt loved when he walked through the front door. The house looked extremely Christmassy. We had put up the tree, decorations and lights.

As the children sat down at the table, one of them said, "Wow! This looks amazing Mum! It looks just like a posh table in a restaurant!"

I could have so easily have missed it. I could have ignored it and hoped that it would go away! I could have not made any effort at all. I could have been miserable. I could have done nothing that would bring any joy to the family.

But that is not me. I was determined that we were going to enjoy the day! I was absolutely determined that Christmas Day was going to be a day filled with joy, hope, love, laughter and fun.

My ex-husband was joining us for lunch; that made me even more determined that the day was going to be a success. It was.

I felt in my heart that I had made considerable progress from last year. That Christmas I could not have sat down to a 'family meal' together. I was still struggling with 'the doorstep' back then.

This Christmas felt different. My heart felt different too. I wanted to bless my ex-husband, my children and our Christmas Day together. I wanted it to go well and for it to be a fun, relaxed day. It was! So much so, that I would consider doing it again.

I wrote in my diary:

> This Christmas has been so nice. I was dreading it. It was the second year of being on my own as a single parent.
>
> I was sure that the children would want to see their Dad on Christmas Day. I was so happy that they were happy and that I had made an effort.

Boxing Day 2011

I got ready early, the children too. I dropped them off at their Dad's. They were going to spend the day with him. It was going to be different from last year. Last year, my ex-husband had created another 'Christmas Day' with roast dinner, stockings and presents. They had had a great time at their Dad's. But as we had all spent Christmas lunch together yesterday I was unsure what their plans would be today.

I spent the day with my Mum and Nan. We had a lovely day together. Three generations sipping cups of tea, talking and laughing together.

I didn't feel the sadness that I felt last Boxing Day. I didn't feel lost. I didn't feel like a 'spare part'. I felt OK. I knew the children would be having a wonderful time with their Dad. I felt happy. I felt relaxed. I enjoyed the day. I wasn't 'trying' to enjoy it; I really loved spending my time with them.

Early that evening I drove to my mother-In-law's house. I knocked on the front door. I was by myself. I didn't feel anxious or worried. I felt really excited that I was going to be seeing everyone.

As I walked into the lounge, I was greeted by my mother-in-law, a second brother-in-law, sister-in-law, nephews and nieces. My ex-husband was also there with our children. I walked into noise and bustle. It was great. Everyone was smiling, talking and laughing. The children were running about. I felt that I belonged.

It was lovely. We had a wonderful evening together.

God has shown me a better way in all of this. God has shown me that love and forgiveness are two of the most crucial keys to personal freedom.

Family is important.

I have discovered that family is what you make it. Family is important. Family is to be valued for what it is. But it also takes effort. When you make really good friends with people that you trust, respect and love, then they become part of your family.

I believe that God has encircled us with an incredible family, made of many different people. Each of them has proved invaluable to us, providing a growing network of love and support, not just for us, but also for one another.

Chapter 14: The Family's Voice

Their Own Stories

This chapter is very different from the rest of this book.

You are about to read real, truthful, honest, heartfelt testimonies from some of my family members and closest friends. These were written towards the end of 2011.

They too have been very deeply affected by my husband walking out of our marriage.

I wonder, had my husband actually taken the time to consider the devastating consequences of adultery, whether he would have embarked on such a journey. I don't know.

I do know that those actions have affected every single member of our extended family and friends in some way or another. It has caused many, if not all, to cry, shake their heads, lose sleep and suffer anguish.

I asked each of them if they would consider writing about how the affair had affected them personally. The only guideline I gave them was to write from their heart whatever they wanted to write. When they may have seemed unsure what to write, I suggested: "Maybe the day they found out that my husband had had an affair?" Or, "How did it affect you personally?" Or, simply, "Whatever is on your heart." It was up to them.

Most were able to write down their thoughts. These I collated. Some took a few weeks, others a few months. It was not an easy task for any of them.

A few found it too difficult to put into words on paper how they felt so we compromised. I sat in front of them with my computer. They talked while I typed. I tried my very best not to influence their words. I wanted it to be their words, not mine.

I had absolutely no idea what each person would say or write. Each person's story was a surprise. Some parts in the stories made me smile and others made my cry.

I am convinced that somewhere in their writing, other hearts will be touched.

This is why I wanted them to have a voice...

* * * * *

Story 1 *(Eldest daughter, age 16)*
When Mum and Dad sat us down on that day, I thought that it was going to be something good. But it turned out to be that Dad had cheated. It felt like a bit of

my heart just went completely. Like there was a hole in my heart. Some bits were missing.

At first I thought Mum and Dad were joking, but then I realised that it was true. That is where my life changed. Dad started to look for another place to live and moved out. I remember Dad packing his things into his car and leaving. I try not to think about it because it always makes me cry. I'm crying now.

When I sat down at the table, I would look over to the place where Dad used to sit, to find nothing but an empty chair. Even now, sometimes I remember all the good times we used to have at the dinner table. Even now, I sometimes look to see the same empty chair. Even as I think about it and write it down, it has made me cry even more.

I miss looking out of the window watching out for Dad. I always used to look for his car pulling into the driveway every evening.

I still remember when I was little. At bedtime, Dad would come into my bedroom pretending to be Puffy the Dragon. He would tell me funny jokes and stories that had happened to him (Puffy) at school. It would always make me laugh! Then he (Puffy) would have to go, because his Mum was making his supper.

That is the Dad he used to be to me. Now, whenever I see him, I hardly recognise him. He is not the same Dad to me. He always used to give each of us a big hug when he came home from work. Now he is not here; it will never be the same.

Every second weekend I go to Dad's place. When I walk in, it doesn't feel like home to me. I always feel as if I need to ask if I want a drink or something to eat. Dad always tells me to help myself, but I feel as if it's not my home.

My life got harder and harder because it tore me apart. It ripped me to pieces. But over the last couple of months it has been getting a little bit easier. My Mum and Dad are not like other parents. They don't argue or shout in front of us. In fact, they don't shout at each other, full stop. They are not enemies – they are friends; they just get along. So I don't have to worry about them fighting. And I don't have to worry about Mum getting hurt.

When it all happened, I forgot one important thing. I have got all my family around me that can help me and support me through it. I also have God. I pray every evening, asking God to bless Dad and our family. Even though Dad has cheated, he is still my Dad and I love him.

I thought I was never going to get over this. But I suppose that you have to move on. Of course, you will never forget about it, but that's life.

* * * * *

Story 2 *(Son, age 15)*

Football: a sport well-known by the whole entire world. It has its ups and downs. Players have affairs and this is what happened to me. Saturday used to be the day I looked forward to all week.

I would wake up at 8am. Papa (Mum's Dad) picked me up at 9am. As I got into the car, he would always say, "Have you got your bag? Have you got your ball? Have you got your towel?"

I would reply, "Yes, I'm ready to go."

We'd set off to the game with Dad waving us off from the front door. We would always arrive 30 minutes early. Papa would always give me a pep talk about what to do and when to do it. The goalkeeper would turn up with his Mum and we would practise in the goal.

I would always score a goal. My mate didn't like that. He would always complain when he didn't save the ball. We would laugh about it. The Manager would turn up and we would all warm up before the game to get our formation ready, to secure our three points before the match.

At the end of the game, Papa and I would always debate over the game. It was fun. Then Papa would always drive us to the bakery and buy sausage rolls for us, and extra for Dad and the girls at home to enjoy. Papa would always stop at the shop and buy me a football magazine.

He'd drop me off at home. Dad would be waiting at the front door for me. He would clap his hands together as I walked up the driveway carrying the food. When I walked into the house, Dad would have fried egg and chips ready for me on the table. Then Dad and I would sit down to watch a football game on television.

As soon as I had eaten, I'd only have half an hour to get ready to go with Papa and Dad to watch our local football team. We were season ticket holders. The girls would spend the afternoon with one of our Grandmas. They took it in turns to look after us while Mum was at work.

We'd step out of the car, which seemed a million miles away. It was really only a short road to the grounds. I guess I was smaller then and everything seemed so much bigger. As we walked along the road, we would play the 'colour shirt' game.

This was a game that Dad and I made up ages ago, when we first started going to football every Saturday afternoon. After we parked the car and started walking towards the stadium, Dad would begin by describing a football kit to me and I would have to guess the team. So Dad would say, "Red and white stripes?" and I would reply, "Sheffield United." Then it was my turn to ask Dad. We played this game every time.

We would get to the ground and feel the excitement of the game. We'd walk through the turnstiles and sit in our seats. Dad and I would always listen to Papa saying who we should sign and the tactics they should play. It was funny. Papa always made Dad and me laugh. On the radio on the way home, we'd listen to the commentary about the game. Papa's suggestions were always right.

I was always excited about spending the day with Papa and Dad. Saturday was my favourite day of the week.

Dad ruined everything and split us all apart.

I now go to Dad's every other weekend, but I no longer have a season ticket and neither does my Dad nor Papa. Instead, Dad has other plans. He meets his girlfriend every other weekend.

Saturday is now just an ordinary day. I miss it the most.

* * * * *

Story 3 *(Youngest daughter, age 13)*
I thought that something funny had happened. I kept asking Dad, "What is it? What is it?"

Mum started crying and Dad was stood next to her while she was sat on the sofa. I said to Dad, "Hug Mum, she's upset." He did it very slowly.

I remember asking Dad what was wrong and he burst into tears. My brother and sister were at Youth Club and he said he would tell me when they got back.

When they got back, he sat us on the sofa and said that he might be moving out. I started crying. We asked, "Why?" He said, "I don't love Mummy any more. I'm in love with someone else."

Then he said, "I need some time to think, so can you give me some space to think about my decision?"

My brother stormed out and Dad said, "Come back," but he kept walking.

I felt very upset and disappointed. I never thought Dad would do this to Mum. I never thought it would end like this.

I always thought we would be a family.

* * * * *

Story 4 *(My Mum)*
The day that I found out that my daughter's marriage was over, I had not long been diagnosed with breast cancer and was waiting to go in for my first operation. I thought that something was wrong, as she and her Dad had been very secretive. But on the Saturday her Dad had said that she needed to come up to tell me something.

I was very angry that they had decided between themselves to keep it from me. After all, she is my daughter and her well-being comes before mine!

Toni and her mother-in-law came to our house. Her mother-in-law seemed a bit apprehensive when she came in. I said to my daughter's mother-in-law that it was not her fault what my son-in-law had done. We have still remained friends ever since.

When I was in hospital, my daughter came to see me with a smile on her face but tears in her eyes and a broken heart, as her world had crashed all around her. Although she kept smiling, I could see that she was hurting but I felt helpless in the hospital bed. My daughter needed me and I could not be there for her.

I was not sure what I was feeling at the time, as all sorts of emotions were going through me at once. I felt angry, disappointed, shattered and very tired. How could my son-in-law do this to her? I had always said that I had the best son-in-law that I could have had.

I have met with my son-in-law on several family occasions since all this has happened. Each meeting gets a little easier. As they say, as time passes, life must go on. He has stuck by his word and is seeing that she is taken care of.

I have watched my daughter grow stronger every day, with her faith and the wonderful friends she has. All have been a constant help. She is coming through the other end.

I wish to say a big thank you to each and every person who has been such a big help to my daughter over this very trying time. You know who you are. Without your help, understanding and faith, I feel things would not be what they are today.

* * * * *

Story 5 *(Dad, 'Papa' to the children)*
Dawn, the morning after my daughter had informed us that her marriage had broken up. Life had just turned another page. Numb. Yes, numb, as there was nothing we could do. After hours of discussions, numerous cups of tea, at the end of the day we just wanted to do something constructive, anything that would make a difference. We are all grown up. We are grandparents. Now was one of those times we wanted to be involved. Just ask us to do anything; that's what grandparents are good at! We have the time. We will find the time.

Let's be clear about the effect this had on all of us. This was a family topic that totally dominated our household daily. As the months unfolded and the legal side was underway, the three children spent every other weekend at their father's, including holiday time.

We see less of our grandchildren now than we did before the separation.

My wife and I enjoyed the children joining us for a trip to the seaside from time to time, staying a night or two at weekends, coming up for lunch, taking my grandson to football, and my wife taking the girls shopping. We offer all of them small jobs to earn pocket money.

Now, both parents jealously guard their weekend time with the children; we understand this. That quality of time has all but gone. Weekends are out of bounds. The school work, plus other activities in the week, have increased; they are growing up. They are teenagers.

My wife and I are both retired, so we have six Saturdays and a Sunday in every week: quality time – time that allows us to be available.

Yes, grandparents are the world's best at being available when family time is at a premium.

We used to just get together with a phone call at short notice. That's what families do. Not now. The children have one weekend at their Mum's and one at their Dad's. This means for us, trying to arrange a family get-together, with all the restrictions it seems to be a waste of effort.

Poem:
Energy and effort is all you need
But just tread carefully and take heed
When emotions and family ties are entwined
Advice is not always accepted, yours or mine
Be disciplined and listen, it's a learning curve
It will just confirm your thoughts, from what you've heard.

* * * * *

Story 6 *(Mother-in-law, Grandma to the children)*
I've been asked to write a few words about my feelings regarding the break-up of my son's marriage.

The first, I think, was shock that it could happen. I remember saying to someone that *they* were not just husband and wife but they were *friends*. Second was anger that he could do such a thing. I can understand an attraction to another person – but letting that attraction develop into something that would destroy a family made me very angry with him.

Then there was guilt. *What had I done wrong?* I must have done *something*. Helplessness was something else that I felt. I just had to stand and watch his wife and children go to hell and back, and there was nothing I could do to ease their pain.

I think for a little while, I must have hated my son; an awful thing to say, but true. I know I shall never have the great relationship that my son and I once had. But things are a little easier for me now but I don't think I shall ever completely forgive him. I know I shall never be able to accept into my life the other woman involved. Having spent a lot of time writing this, I still don't think I have expressed my feelings very well. I have found it very difficult to write even these few lines.

I'm glad that I have still got a wonderful daughter-in-law and such lovely grandchildren in my life. It could so easily have been very different.

* * * * *

Story 7 *(Nan)*
I didn't like to see my great-grandchildren upset and I didn't like to see my granddaughter so unhappy. I didn't like that.

My great-grandson seemed to be quite angry and seemed to take it out on his sister quite a bit. I didn't like to see that either. I feel that it affected him more than the others. He lost his football, his training, and going to the match with his Dad and Granddad, which seemed to make him angry. Things seem to have settled down now.

I can't say that I feel my ex-grandson-in-law has been generous: he only took his responsibilities as he should have done. He shouldn't have left the children at such tender ages. It would have been better waiting until they were older and had left school. He's tried to do his best but I felt that it was a very bad thing for him to leave the children at the ages that they were. It was just too soon. It affected their school work and their general attitude to things around them. It made them completely unsettled.

It's one of those things that seem to be happening all too often these days. In a marriage, I feel that if there is something wrong, people should talk about it, not go off with someone else.

I think Toni has handled it far better than most people inasmuch as it hasn't affected the children as it might have done, because she has kept everything on an even keel.

* * * * *

Story 8 *(Great Aunt and great-great-aunt and godparent to the children)*
How did I feel? Sad: so sad for Toni, her husband, and the children. They always seemed such a happy family. I've never, ever heard them quarrel.

A few weeks before, we had all gone out for dinner to celebrate Toni's 40th birthday and everything seemed normal. I know none of us know what is round the corner, but I just hope that the worst is now over for them all. From now on, it will be plain sailing – God willing.

* * * * *

Story 9 *(Close friend, and the children's godparent)*
It was some time since I had spoken with or seen Toni, her husband and my godchildren. I felt guilty and knew that I needed to ring them, because it had been so long.

The phone rang. I could see who was calling. My heartbeat quickened and I pondered, not answering the phone for a moment, but that served no purpose as I really wanted to speak to them and see them. It was a horrible thought but I picked up the phone all cheerful and happy. Then I heard Toni say, "I have something to tell you."

She said that she and her husband were going to separate. I was speechless! *Beyond* speechless. Toni was talking to me but I was not hearing what was being said. My mind was all over the place. *No! I didn't hear that right! She didn't say that! What did she just say?* I thought to myself. *They are separating? He's had an affair? No! NEVER!*

I thought I KNEW him really well! I was so flabbergasted. I quickly accepted that I needed to give her some space. We hung up the phone.

I burst into tears and sobbed uncontrollably. I struggled to understand what I had just heard.

I was distraught and I couldn't stop crying. I really, really couldn't believe it. If ever there were any couple that I thought were in love and would be together for ever, it was *them*.

I had a terrible night's sleep that night and I worried about Toni and the children for days. I now question why I never worried about *him* throughout all of this.

The whole family held a very special place in my heart

Toni is quite a religious person and weeks later she kept telling me that she had forgiven him for what he had done and would still like him back. I could not understand this. Right from the very beginning of the situation, she had forgiven him. I was astounded that she could do this so early after it all came out. She believed in certain values, but she was still a long way from 'healing' over what had happened.

I was quite surprised that Toni suddenly announced that she wanted a divorce – once she had made up her mind, there was no going back.

Toni, my heart goes out to you throughout all of this. You have kept your dignity and spirits up in the face of a very personal situation and I know that you have always had the interests of the children first and foremost in your mind.

Love is a very varied thing and you know that we will always be there for you. I love you all.

* * * * *

Story 10 *(Close friend)*
When Toni asked me to write something for this book, the first thought that came to mind was – "Awesome!" Toni's favourite word.

The day that I found out that Toni's husband had been having an affair was a school day. I knocked on her front door as usual to walk up to school with her and the children. She was always late. But this particular morning, she opened the door and said, "Sorry, we are running late. I will see you later."

As I walked up to school, that was playing on my mind. So I walked my dog quickly around the block and when I got home I phoned her straightaway.

She broke down in tears on the phone.

I went straight down to her house. She told me that her husband had been having an affair. It was just like a dream, a bad dream. I thought they had the perfect marriage. They were always meeting for lunch, going out for evenings together and he even took her to Amsterdam for her 40th birthday as a surprise.

We sat talking, crying and laughing over a cup of tea. When I found out about all this, I too was going through a separation from my husband.

Whilst I had been going through a separation from my husband, she had been going through all of this by herself! She had been there for me, she had been my shoulder to cry on. Toni was a diamond of a friend.

Toni had her faith in God which I felt gave her the strength to get through it. She also had her family and her friends.

I just can't believe the way that Toni has handled this chapter in her life. She seemed so calm about it, just her normal self – well, normal for Toni! She hadn't told me anything.

It was weird afterwards. Most people would scream, shout, throw away their husband's clothes! But not Toni. She even helped her husband find a flat!

See, that is what makes Toni special. She always sees the good in people, even when they have hurt her.

As I live only a few doors away, our doors are always open for each other. The amount of tea we have gone through has been huge. As time has gone on, we have all become closer. Toni and her children are like my extended family. Even her family are like my extended family also.

When someone leaves the house, the dinner table becomes empty. It's only one person but it feels like more – so cooking becomes fast food meals. So, over a cuppa one day, we decided to cook a roast dinner for each other and our children, once a month. We took it in turns to provide the pudding and then we would all wash up afterwards. It was awesome.

Christmas and our birthdays were coming up too. So over another cuppa we decided we Mums wanted stockings to open on Christmas morning too. I took Toni's children into town so that they could buy their Mum presents, and she took mine. It has now become like a tradition.

As Toni had had a difficult year and her 41st birthday was coming up, Toni's Mum and I organised a surprise birthday for her. It was a really good night and I think she was surprised.

The journey over the last two years has had its highs and lows. But one thing I am really grateful for is that Toni and her children are part of our lives. She is my very best friend whom I love dearly. We have had so many good memories, such as long shopping trips, family parties, bike rides and endless cups of tea around the kitchen table. Hopefully there are many more to come.

I love you, Toni.

* * * * *

Story 11 *(Close 'Irish' friend)*

My first impression was of a secure, very attractive family with ready smiles. They were very open about their family life.

We started to build a friendship before the end of 2009. That is when Toni began to share her concerns about her husband's strange behaviour.

Although my natural inclination was to think that her husband was having an affair, Toni's confidence that he wasn't, made me think that he was just going through a bad patch. Unfortunately as it turned out, Toni discovered that he actually was having an affair.

She was always such a strong character. She never once blamed God and held strong to her faith.

She demonstrated such strength of character giving security to the children.

During the first few days of him moving out, Toni was determined to walk with God and to offer reconciliation if there was genuine repentance. But it never came.

During this time, the strength of Toni's faith was amazing. Her ability to walk in truth, even though in deep sorrow, was a reflection of her character. Along with this, she was always agonising over making the right, godly decision.

I have grown to love this woman who has become an example to those around. She is a wonderful example of how to walk through the 'Valley of Betrayal'.

* * * * *

Story 12 *(Close friend)*

Prayer is a Powerful Tool

As she laid her heart bare again, just between the two of us, late one night, I felt an urgency in my spirit to fast and pray. We found a week in our diaries when, each day, we could fast and get together for a few hours to pray,

It was a powerful time to stand with my friend whom I loved dearly, in the toughest season of her life: to come together in powerful prayers of agreement; to encourage her through deeply painful times with the Word of God and God's promises.

Prayer is not the last resort; it is the most powerful tool, and I know one it's which makes her strong in Christ. When the tornado of infidelity tore through her life, it didn't take her out: it made her strong as she stood on the Rock of Jesus Christ.

* * * * *

Story 13 *(Close friend)*

I met Toni in 2000. We used to go to the local toddler group that used to meet once a week in the mornings, over the road from where I lived. As the toddler group didn't start until later, Toni and another friend of ours used to come back to my house for a cup of tea first. I got to know her really well and she became my best friend.

When everything came out in the open about him having an affair, it was such an excruciatingly painful time for her and all who were close to her.

As a God-fearing woman, Toni was very gracious in her dealings with her husband and was quick to forgive him. Nevertheless, he still chose to leave.

In the days since Toni's husband left, things have not been easy for her, but the Lord Jesus is her constant source of strength and encouragement.

May what she's written help many who find themselves travelling similar paths.

* * * * *

Story 14 *(Brother-in-law, and godparent to the children)*
To be honest, it didn't come as a total surprise when I heard that Toni and my brother were no longer together, although the circumstances did.

Toni looked really sad and not herself when I last saw them together, the Christmas before they separated (2009).

However, when the news broke, there was never a moment when I thought that Toni and the children would not be part of the family any more. And although no discussion of this nature took place, I am one hundred per cent sure my mother and brothers thought the same. It was important to Toni to still feel part of the family and I hope she still feels that she is.

I still consider Toni as my sister-in-law and it goes without question that I am uncle to their three children.

I'm glad to see Toni is happy again and has a strong circle of friends, and seems to draw a lot of strength through her faith in God. Long may that continue.

* * * * *

Story 15 *(Close friend – Pastor's wife)*
Toni had asked to see my husband and me with a pastoral issue. My husband is the Senior Minister of the church Toni attends, and on another level we were also friends with both Toni and her husband. Our children were also friends with each other. Although her husband did not share our faith, we all enjoyed each other's company and had mutual respect for one another.

One Saturday morning I had a phone call from Toni. She was clearly distraught and explained to me that she had found a letter from another woman to her husband. The content of the letter made it clear they were having an affair. I went to her house straightaway as she was there on her own with the children, as her husband had gone away for a few days. As she showed me the letter, I felt so sad for my friend. Toni is a very attractive, bright, bubbly, passionate, caring person. She always remains positive. She is very talented and extremely dignified, a quality that she has carried throughout this turmoil.

I took the children home to allow Toni to begin dealing with the immediate circumstances. I remember, I tried to cheer the children up and distract them from wondering what was going on but they looked at me and asked, "What's wrong with Mum? Has someone died?" For a split second I felt relieved that I could say no-one had died, but I knew I could not say that everything would be alright (the words children are supposed to hear from an adult when things go wrong). I just said, "Mum will explain everything later." I don't know if the children will remember that day. They had so many darker moments to face, but for me that summed up the overall depth of despair of this situation.

As I have watched and supported Toni through the pain and sadness, I have great admiration for her. She has been tried and tested and has come out on top. Toni has kept God at the centre of her being. She is a pillar of strength for her children and they have learned so much about love and forgiveness from her.

* * * * *

Story 16 *(Close friends)*
We left the UK in May 2009 having been good friends with Toni for what really seems a lifetime! Words could not describe, and our hearts could hardly contain, the news which we received only a few months later.

I believe our God is a God of restoration and He will refill your lives with the desires of your hearts.

For you to come to a point of recovery, re-establishing yourself while holding tight to the things you hold so dear, is nothing short of miraculous.

You are a role model to us both and we admire your guts, steadfastness and childlike faith. We are forever rooting for you.

* * * * *

Story 17 *(Close friend)*
Each conversation we have had over the two years has been about the goodness of God that Toni has been experiencing every day, rather than ugliness. She still talks almost lovingly about her husband, and never once has she given me any reason to be bitter towards him. She is indeed a woman who seeks after God's heart and still loves even when she has been so hurt.

I remember she once said, "I don't want my heart to be cold, because that's not me." All she desired was to love and keep on loving regardless. I cannot recall Toni ever uttering an ugly word, not that she hasn't been angry or felt bitter, but she seemed to make a choice to love through it all. Even when I have been lost for words, Toni fills the gap by recalling the beauty of God.

She held on to God with hope, yet not everything turned out the way she would have loved. Instead, she waded through the storm and kept her eyes on God. She was positive and hopeful during the down times and the up times, smiling through it all. She made a conscious effort to remain hopeful and not to be bitter.

Toni, you are a woman after my heart and a minister of the love of God. You radiate His love to all those around you and you are loved so dearly. No doubt, God will carry you through the journey ahead.

* * * * *

Story 18 *(Close friends)*
We always knew Toni and her husband as a solid and strong couple with their wonderful children but we began to notice some little cracks in their relationship. It began when we met together at our house a few days before Christmas 2009. We thought that whatever the issue was, it would be resolved. We didn't know how deep the crisis was.

So, when we heard about their separation it really was a shock. We hoped they would get back together.

It was very distressing and painful for her to become a single mother in a matter of a few days. When we spent time together talking, it seemed Toni was trying hard to keep things as simple as possible for the sake of the children. When we heard the news of their divorce, we saw her fighting hard to keep the children from being exposed to what would have been a heavier and more painful blow to their lives.

We have witnessed Toni go through different stages – from being totally lost, angry, tearful, full of fear and emotionally vulnerable, to slowly and steadily rebuilding her life, accepting the fact that there would be no more life 'together'.

Fast forward to March 2012. When walking through Toni's front door, we had the feeling of a very warm house, united and closer. To see and experience the relaxed atmosphere with the two new kittens cuddled up in front of the fire with the children, their mum in the kitchen warming up pains au chocolat, seemed the beginning of a new chapter in their lives.

We left their house and our hearts felt light and lifted. We hope you all have a wonderful life!

* * * * *

To My Children, Family and Close Friends:
Thank you for contributing to this chapter of the book. Your stories have amazed me. I know how painstakingly difficult it was for each of you to write but I thank you for it. I pray that through your boldness and courageous hearts,

many people will be able to identify with what you have written. I hope and pray that people are blessed by your stories as much as they have blessed me.

In Addition – To My Family and Close Friends:

Thank you, for every reassuring hug, every prayer; every text or phone call checking to see how we are. For all the times we have chatted over a cup of tea, of which there have been many! Thank you for believing in me; listening to me and especially – for not giving up on me.

Thank you for everything! Thank you for your love and support. Thank you for always being there for us, encouraging us, building us up and, most importantly, making us laugh. I know it has been a tough, painful road for each one of us, but when I think of you all, I smile. In amongst the tears and heartache, we have shared together many times of joy and laughter. Thank you for helping me and my children to laugh again.

Each one of you is precious to me. You are wonderful. I thank God that He has put each of you in our lives and I pray that God will bless you abundantly.

I love you with all my heart!

Toni x

Chapter 15: Walking in Victory

Stepping out of One Life into Another

November 2011

I t is now November 2011. One year and nine months has passed since my husband left me for another woman. It doesn't sound like a long time, but it has felt like a lifetime. The trauma was very sudden and the impact on me and my children was severe. Becoming a single parent has been a difficult adjustment, a stark contrast to my former life.

> *Jeremiah 29:11-12*
> *(11) "For I know the plans I have for you," declares the Lord, "plans to prosper you and not to harm you, plans to give you hope and a future. (12) Then you will call upon me and come and pray to me, and I will listen to you. (13) You will seek me and find me when you seek me with all your heart."*

I have held on very tightly to this scripture. I have prayed it endlessly. I have said it aloud so many times, I have lost count. It hangs on a little plaque in my porch. It was a present from my Mum many months ago. The impact and power behind the words in the scripture has made a difference to my life. I believe the words and I thank God that He has a plan for our lives.

When I felt so worthless and low, this scripture enabled me to face the day with renewed hope and faith. God has a purpose for my life. I haven't been in a position to see exactly what God's *plan* is, but I *have* held on to those words with sincere determination.

When I have felt a sudden wave of emotion flood over me at work, I have quietly locked myself into the bathroom cubicle and thanked God that he *has a plan for me*. It seems rather pathetic writing it down on paper, but that is the truth of it. In those moments I have needed to pray.

God has a plan. God has a purpose. There is hope in God. There is peace in God. When everything around me collapsed, the walls felt as if they were closing in and my heart was in a mess; God stayed right by my side.

My life wasn't meant to turn out this way. I was abandoned and left unloved by a husband whom I had loved for nearly twenty years.

It had been such a difficult journey, one of great pain, suffering and anguish. Now I was about to face a new chapter in my life.

5th November 2011

I thought it was going to be an ordinary day. I had been invited to attend my friend's firework party that evening. I spent the morning loading and unloading tables and chairs ready for the party. I began singing a song. It was a song thanking God for His love for me.

In the afternoon, after I had helped my friend, I went home. I opened the front door and I picked up the post. I walked into the lounge and dropped the envelopes onto the coffee table. I walked back into the porch, took off my shoes and put on my slippers. I dumped my bag on the floor and looked again at the pile of letters on the table.

There was an envelope on the top of the pile. I could tell from the stamp on the front that it was from my solicitor. I opened it. The words jumped off the page.

"… please find enclosed a copy of your Decree Absolute …"

"Oh," I said aloud to the room.

It was unexpected. I thought it would be nearer to Christmas, a few more weeks yet. It was quite a shock.

All I could see was the words: "You are officially divorced."

"Oh," I said again into the air. I breathed a long sigh.

The paper was very plain, only one sheet and it didn't look anything spectacular.

Then I realised something important … I felt OK. I really did. *I felt OK!*

I didn't feel tearful, and I didn't need to sit down. Instead, a smile broke out over my face. I was suddenly struck by the realisation of what it meant.

In a few hours I would be attending the party with my *now* ex-husband, my children, my Mum, and my best friend. We would be attending it together!

Many times I had wondered what I would *feel* like at the exact moment of opening *that* letter.

Would I cry or crumple in a heap? How would I feel? How would I react?

I didn't feel any negative things.

> *Proverbs 16:3*
> *Commit to the Lord whatever you do, and your plans will succeed.*

Instead of crying as I thought I would, I began singing praises to God. I stood there alone in my lounge, singing the song that had been on my heart all day. I realised that God had given me a new song. It was incredible! On the day of my divorce, I was singing a new song with a heart of joy.

God *has* a *future* for me! A *plan* for me! God loves me!

I stood there smiling and reflecting on the last few months. God had been slowly teaching me the benefits of being amicable with my ex-husband, even in the little things.

A fresh word

A few weeks later I was at church one evening. During worship God gave me a picture and a word. It stayed with me all evening.

The word was:

> Are you ready to climb? If you are, you need to be ready to jump!

I then saw a picture of an indoor swimming pool. Above the pool were three diving boards. One was low, the other medium-high, and the third was very high.

I wrote in my diary that evening:

> In order to climb, I need to follow God and not my own agenda.
> I must trust God and not look down, but look to God.
>> I do not need to fear. I need to listen to God's voice and be obedient to God.
>> Climbing takes courage, energy and faith; faith that I will not fall.

I thought about that picture for a while that evening. It always amazes me how much God knows me. He knows that I would never attempt to dive off any of the diving boards, and more importantly, I would most certainly not consider diving off the top one.

I don't much like heights. I went bungee jumping in New Zealand fourteen years ago with my friend when I returned there for a brief holiday. I had always wanted to try it.

I was excited when the instructors put the rope around my ankles. I thought it would be *so* easy. I imagined that I would walk out onto the platform and fling myself forward; arms outstretched and enjoy the experience.

But no! It didn't happen as I imagined. My friend who I was with, had absolutely no fear of heights whatsoever. She gestured for me to go first, because she knew that I might not go through with it.

Well, it all looked exciting. There was an intense atmosphere up there on that ridge. We waited in line. People seemed to jump off without hesitation.

Then it was my turn. As I stood up, I was surprised how heavy the rope was around my ankles, it seemed to weigh a ton. I shuffled forward towards the jumping area. *That is when I realised what I was doing!* I held onto the rail very tightly as I inched my way forward. Then suddenly the handrail stopped. It didn't go right to the very edge. I looked down at the floor. In front of me was the painted picture of two enlarged feet with the toes close to the edge. I knew that that was where I was meant to put my feet, but I completely froze to the spot. Rooted like a statue.

My friend cheered me on. So did other people behind me. The instructor held out his hands and encouraged me to place my hands in his. I took my hands off the rail. I shuffled forward some more until my toes were right on the edge.

I looked down. That was a big mistake. My heart was going overtime. There I was, standing with a rope around my ankles, on the edge of a ridge with nothing to hold onto! *What was I doing?*

I could see the lake below me, it looked beautiful. Directly below me was a man in a little rowing boat. He was calling up to me, encouraging me to jump, *but he seemed so far away*!

Fear and terror filled my entire body. *I can't do it! I can't jump! What am I doing?* The people behind me were still encouraging me: "Jump!" "Go on, you can do it! Jump." Easy for them to say! They couldn't see what I could see! It was such a long way down! Long, long way down! I scrunched my eyes shut!

That was not helping! I was shaking! I couldn't move. The thought of falling forwards was *absolutely* terrifying! So I stood there. I stood there. I stood there!

By now forty minutes had passed. The people behind me had given up encouraging me and moved on to telling me to "Hurry up!" They were getting rather annoyed at this point.

The instructor tried to tell me to let someone else have a turn and sit down for a while. But I couldn't move. My legs were like jelly.

I kept saying to him, "I'm going to do it. I'm not going all the way back to the UK and telling my family that I came all the way here and didn't do it!" I was standing there shaking and now my head was going from side to side as well. I looked at him – "No. No. No," I said. "I have to do it!"

This was all in the midst of now agitated voices in the background.

I'm not sure but I think the instructor felt sorry for me. Then he said, "If you turn around and hold my hands, I'll lean you backwards level to the ridge. Then I'll let you go. That will be better."

I looked at him. This was the only way I was going to leave this ridge. I was not quitting. *I was not.* I just couldn't look down. So maybe leaning backwards would be better. I looked again down at the lake and the man in the boat. He too had given up encouraging me and looked bored just sitting there.

"OK," I said. He helped me turn around. He held my hands. He then told me to inch backwards slightly so only my toes were on the edge. I did. Then he lowered me backwards.

He looked me straight in the eye and held me there for a moment. I didn't know in that split second what was more terrifying. Standing up looking down at the boat or looking into his eyes knowing there was no way back to safety. The only way was down. I had no control. "Bye," he said. Then he let go.

I screamed all the way to the bottom. The man in the boat carefully undid the rope from my ankles and lowered me safely into the boat.

I had done it! Within minutes, my friend did the perfect bungee jump. She let herself fall forward and looked fantastic. It was just as if she had done it many times before.

As she joined me in the boat, I said, "I'd like to do that again! That was good!"

"No!" she said laughing. The man in the boat also quickly said, "No, they only let you do it once!" Forty-five minutes it had taken me. Forty-five minutes I had stood there absolutely terrified. I couldn't say that I actually bungee jumped. I had cheated really. But I was determined not to quit.

So when God showed me that picture, I sat back and thought about it. God knows that for me to dive off the top diving board would be just as terrifying.

I believe that God doesn't make us go to the top diving board first. He takes us through each step. In order to jump off the top board we need to be confident at jumping off the lower boards first.

I believe that God does not rush us either. God is a God who loves us, cares for us and wants to nurture us and guide us. I believe God is a God who wants good things for us.

I certainly do not recommend anyone to go bungee jumping. Quite the opposite actually. It is something I never, ever plan to repeat. Not ever!

I feel that God has taken me on a journey. One of forgiveness. One of hope. One of love. One of faith and one of humility.

If I had not chosen to forgive my ex-husband before he walked out on our marriage, I don't think that it would have been possible for me to find a place of being amicable with him so quickly. Forgiving him has been a process.

Inviting him into our home for a cup of tea meant that we were able to begin a journey of resolving 'the doorstep' issues. Making an extra effort to walk with a good attitude and to speak with kind words has meant that we have been able to go to family functions and school appointments with a heart of unity and love.

This has all impacted our children and our extended family in such positive ways.

My daughter challenged me just the other day. I was typing her piece of writing for this book and she said that it was good that her Dad and I are friends.

I met him for lunch in town a few days later. We were sitting at this little rickety metal round table that wobbled if you leant on it too hard with your elbow. I was sitting on an uncomfortable flat cushion on top of a boxed-in seat against the wall. He was sitting in a little chair that matched the table. Old pictures hung on the wall behind me. People sat next to us on either side. There was little space as the tables and chairs were packed tightly together.

As I looked up, I thought about what she had said. Were we friends? It was difficult to answer. I looked at him. I looked at us. I was very aware that we were sitting having lunch together and enjoying each other's company. It was relaxing. We were laughing together. We always used to get on so well when we were married. Now things are different, but over the last few months we have got on a lot better.

So there I sat, in what had become our 'usual' coffee shop. I remembered how nervous I had been the first time I had met him there for lunch. But today was different. We had crossed over so many hurdles and climbed so many mountains of grief since then.

I looked at him. I looked into his eyes. That statement from my daughter played on my mind. He was always kind and helpful if I or the children needed anything. He had been incredibly gracious and amicable going through the divorce proceedings. He had always been very generous-hearted when it came to the children. He had always kept to the childcare arrangements, and lately the children had been seeing more of their Dad as we were much more relaxed about everything.

We had a history together. We were Mum and Dad to our children. Looking back at all that we had gone through in such a short space of time, it was I believe by God's grace and nothing short of a miracle that we had become friends and that there was no disunity between our families.

26th January 2012

I wrote in my diary:

> Dear Heavenly Father, Mighty God, Mighty King, Everlasting Father. My Lord, my Saviour, my Friend. Thank you for holding my hand. Thank you for being with me every second of every day. Thank you for hearing my heart's cry; for wiping every tear; for healing my broken heart; for restoring my heart, my family and my home.
>
> Mould me, shape me, and refine me. Help me to be the woman of God you are calling me to be. Help me to walk with a heart of love every day. I surrender all I am to you. Thank you for loving me.

God told me to trust Him five days before I found the evidence that my husband was having an affair. That was twenty-two months ago.

Now God is showing me a picture of a swimming pool. First I need to dive off the edge of the pool before I move onto the lowest diving board. I can do that. Whatever *that* is.

> *Psalm 62:1-2*
> *(1) My soul finds rest in God alone; my salvation comes from him. (2) He alone is my rock and my salvation; he is my fortress, I shall never be shaken.*

I am ready, and my heart is ready. I feel peace in my heart and I can smile. It could have all been very different. I could have chosen not to listen to God. I could have lost my dear friends through bitterness and anger. I could have lost my extended family on my ex-husband's side. Our home could have been filled with tension. My relationship between my ex-husband and me could have been full of anger and hatred causing much friction.

I praise God that instead, I won the battle. We won the battle together as a family!

There is no disunity between my ex-husband and me; therefore the children, who are now teenagers, have the freedom to see their Dad whenever they like, in an atmosphere of amicability, unity and love.

Our home is full of love, unity, honesty and joy. Our lounge and kitchen seem to be constantly flowing with family, friends, neighbours, extended family and food.

We adore our two soppy cats that spend their days being carried about, sleeping and delivering us mice and worms. This causes much uproar, calamity and laughter.

So considering all that I have been through, and where I am now – I feel confident to say that I am standing in a place of victory and I am very excited about my future.

Even though it has been difficult and challenging at times to put my pride and hurting heart to one side, God has shown me that He has a better way.

* * * * *

The reason I have poured out my heart and soul and revealed my inmost secrets is that I would like to make this very personal to you...

Chapter 16: Saying Goodbye

Taking a Brave Step

January 2013

> *2 Corinthians 1: 3-4*
> *Praise be to the God and Father of our Lord Jesus Christ, the Father of compassion and the God of all comfort, who comforts us in all our troubles, so that we can comfort those in any trouble with the comfort we ourselves have received from God.*

A few days after Christmas Day 2012, I received a phone call from my Nan. She asked me if I would visit her the following evening.

My Nan lived with my Mum and Dad. They had lived together for more than twenty years, and their house was only five minutes down the road. As I put the phone down, I knew that it was not going to be good news as Nan had not been herself lately. She had been feeling a little unwell for the past few months.

The next evening, my youngest daughter and I knocked on their front door. Nan ushered us inside and made us all a cup of tea. She seemed rather quiet. We carried our cups into the lounge and put them down onto the dining table, whilst my daughter stayed in the kitchen chatting with my Mum.

As we sat down, Nan reached for my hand and said very gently and quietly, "The doctor has told me I have pancreatic cancer. There is nothing they can do. It is inoperable."

I felt myself gripping her hand tighter as she spoke. "Oh Nan," I said. *I didn't know what to say. What could I say?* As I looked into her eyes, I reached my arms out to her and hugged her. I kept saying over and over, "I love you, Nan. I love you, Nan. I love you so much, Nan."

She was *my* Nan. She had been there for me through every step of my life. I loved her so much. She was the person who had always encouraged me the most. Ever since I was a little girl she had taken the time to sit with me, laugh with me and listen to me. She was the person I trusted and confided in with everything. She would always tell me straight what she thought and it didn't matter if I didn't agree; we would sit for hours laughing and discussing life's issues.

I was still in shock. My head was leaning against hers as my right arm draped over her thin shoulders. She was so tiny, even smaller in stature than me. We both sat staring at the table cloth with our heads hung low. The news was difficult to take in. The severity of it was even worse.

This wasn't any *ordinary* cancer; this was *inoperable* cancer. Nan explained to me that the doctors could offer no treatment, except to make her as comfortable as possible.

Then I said, "Nan, let's pray." She nodded, "OK," she said. As I began to pray, tears ran down our cheeks. *This was the first time Nan had ever agreed to me praying for her.*

When we left my Mum and Dad's house that evening, I knew in my heart that I wanted to write Nan a letter. I wanted her to know how much I loved her and to thank her for everything she had done for me over the years. After much writing and rewriting, I put the letter in an envelope two weeks later. I sealed it and wrote on the front: "Nan, from me to you." Later that evening we visited briefly and whilst she was downstairs in her chair, I snuck upstairs into her bedroom and placed it on her pillow.

This is what it said:

> Dear Nan
>
> Thank you for being my Nan. I love you so very much.
>
> For as long as I can remember, you have always been there for me.
>
> You have always made me feel so special, loved and cherished. We have always been close.
>
> When I sat and held your hand that day at the table only a few weeks ago, the words "I love you" didn't seem enough. So I wanted to write a few words on paper that would express my heart better. My intention is not to make you cry, but somewhere amidst our tears, to make you smile.
>
> I have always been able to talk to you about anything; and to share my heart honestly and openly with you. We have spent much time over the years talking and laughing together over a cup of tea. Ever since I was young, you have had this ability to make me feel like you believed in me, no matter what. Even when I have made mistakes, you continued to encourage me and spur me on.
>
> You are such an inspiration to me. You have an extremely positive attitude to life, people, and situations which arise. Rather than speaking negatively, your words are filled with gentleness, wisdom and hope.
>
> You have a quiet and gentle nature, yet a boldness and courageous spirit. You are never afraid to speak your mind or to say what you really think. Your words may at times be

few, but more often than that, direct and to the point. I've always loved that about you.

I love your giggle. It makes me smile just thinking about it. You find the goodness and sense of humour in most situations. You have an incredible knack of finding the fun in most conversations. When you start giggling, your shoulders start shaking; eyes start watering; and you can't stop smiling. Your giggle is infectious. It makes everyone else start laughing too. That is what I love about you the most.

You have such a gentle, caring nature. Recently you said to me, "Try always to say yes. Only when you really can't say yes, only then, say no. But do try to say yes." What an incredible statement! One I don't always manage to follow, but one which I'm always trying to adopt.

You tirelessly give to others; putting their needs before your own. You always consider other people's feelings and put everyone else first, before yourself. You hardly ever grumble or complain and will rarely mention your own troubles or woes. Instead you sit quietly, smiling and being cheerful.

Even as a young child, to this present day, you make me feel like you have all the time in the world for me. You have shown me such compassion, patience and love. Your ear is always keen to listen attentively, kindly and lovingly – even from long distances! Do you remember when you came running down the path to the park and rescued my friend and me; terrified and clinging for dear life on top of that climbing frame in the park? There was a vicious dog barking at us. All we kept yelling at the top of our voices was … "NANNY!" It was a miracle that you heard us that day. But I still remember it clearly. I have never been so glad to see you!

When I used to stay at your house at the weekends, it was my favourite time of the week. I would wake up early in the morning and reach my arm up and onto the bedside table. There, without fail, would be a round container and a drink. I wouldn't even sit up. Instead I would open the lid and dunk my biscuits into my drink and eat every one. Mornings were one of my favourite times of the day. Afterwards, I would go back to sleep. When I woke up, there would be the smell of bacon and sausages – Granddad's breakfast.

As a child, I remember you and Granddad playing cards with me for what seemed like hours. I tried to win; you would let me; but Granddad would not. "She has to win on her own merit," he would say. As you looked in dismay, you would say, "Oh, just let her win one game." I very rarely won, but when I did win, it felt great. I'm afraid to say that I have carried on that same tradition towards my children, much to their dismay.

Then came the evenings. We would sit and wait patiently. You or Granddad would disappear into the kitchen and bring into the lounge three little side plates. Each carried the long-awaited chocolate squares. If I remember correctly, those plates only ever carried eight each; no more than eight was allowed; and 'seconds' were forbidden: those were for the next evening. The eight squares were not stuck together, but were meticulously broken up into individual squares and spread out onto the plates: always milk chocolate. We made them last as long as possible and savoured each one. They tasted more delicious somehow than if we had eaten the whole slab (although I never had the opportunity to test this theory).

I was so fortunate to spend the weekends with you and Granddad. I loved it. You both always made me feel special.

Then came the day when you began to look after my eldest daughter when I went to work part-time. I still have the photo of you sitting on the couch in the front room. I came to collect her one day when she was only little. As I peered around the door, there you sat: bike helmet on your head, knee pads on your knees; and elbow pads on both elbows; smiling and listening to her as she was intently talking and giggling with you. It was a beautiful sight. Nothing is ever too much trouble for you.

One day we popped in to see you. I had telephoned first to see if you were home. When we arrived and walked through the front door and into the kitchen, a sea of cakes was before us. I remember it, so clearly. We had only rung two hours before: fairy cakes, butterfly cakes, fruit loaf and scones lined the kitchen work surfaces. "Help yourself," you said. I stood amazed not only at how many cakes you had made in such a short space of time, but that you had gone to the trouble of making all those cakes for us.

You are the most wonderful person I know. The kindest, most loving, generous-hearted person I know. We all love you, Nan, so very much. You have taught me so much over the years. Thank you for loving me. Thank you for loving us.

You have not only been my Nan, but a Nan to many others. When I was growing up, all my friends called you Nan too. You have enlightened and enriched many people's lives Nan, and continue to do so each day.

I hope that one day, when my children have their own children; I will be the kindest and loving Nanny to their children that you have always been to me.

Much love to you,

Toni x

PS: Enclosed is a little booklet one of my best friends gave to me on 2nd November 2001, over ten years ago. That was the year that I invited Jesus into my heart; and from that very moment, God changed my life. I love you Nan; so does God. He loves you abundantly and exuberantly more.

As I crept down the stairs, I still felt rather nervous. *What would she think when she read the letter? What would she say? What would she think of the booklet? I had never given her a Christian booklet about Jesus before.*

I needn't have worried, she thought it was lovely. In fact, she read it to my Mum and Great Aunt, so that was a good sign. A few days later, I summoned up the courage to ask her if she had read the little booklet, and her reply was, "Well, yes, I had a look at it." *I wasn't quite sure from her response if she was totally in favour of the booklet or not.*

One or two Sundays later, my Nan, great-aunt, Mum, youngest daughter and I walked through the doors of Nan's parish church. She hadn't attended for a while and felt it was time to go back. As we walked down the aisle to find a seat, Nan and my great-aunt were greeted by many of the parishioners, many of whom were friends.

We chose a wooden pew near the middle of the church and filed in one by one. When we sat down, we were very aware that we were five generations sitting together. Many people came up to us and commented on that fact, which made us all smile.

During the service I helped Nan walk to the front of the church so she could take part in communion. Afterwards we walked back to our seats and I struggled to hold back the tears. I glanced at Nan, who being very frail was holding my arm. I could see that she was smiling. I was intrigued.

When I visited Nan the next day, she told me what had happened.

"I made my peace with God," she said, grinning.

"Really, what do you mean?" I asked curiously.

"Well, when I knelt at the altar and took communion, I prayed," she said.

She continued to tell me more, and as she was talking, her face was beaming with the biggest smile.

I knew that it had taken a great deal of courage for her to go to church. She had been upset with God for a long time. But not any more!

In fact, she was so happy!

She said that she felt *different* too. She said that she felt *lighter*. She said that she should have gone to church years ago and not waited so long! She looked radiant and noticeably more peaceful.

I asked her what she had prayed. She simply said that she had asked God to forgive her for being angry at Him, and for not going to church for a long time. She said that she asked God to look after her and to look after her family.

Sadly, that was the first and last visit to church we made together. We tried several times to plan another trip, but Nan was not well enough.

March 2013

At the end of March, three months after being diagnosed with pancreatic cancer, Nan turned ninety years old. She was not able to get out of bed at this stage, so all the family gathered in her bedroom upstairs. We sat chatting and laughing. Nan sat up in bed and enjoyed her day. We sang her *Happy Birthday*, helped her open her presents and we all ate birthday cake together. It was lovely.

The children and I visited Nan nearly every single day. So did family, friends, neighbours and nurses. Mum and Dad's house was constantly full of people.

We sat for hours talking with Nan, reading to her, and reminiscing about the past. After her birthday she was moved to a hospital bed downstairs. The front lounge became her bedroom.

Nan loved to laugh. We would chuckle over funny stories that had happened years before. Every day it was wonderful to see her, but it was heartbreaking to see her get weaker and weaker.

She was the kindest, sweetest person and she never stopped smiling.

April 2013

A few days before my Nan passed away, I quietly walked into her room and gently took hold of her hand. Whilst standing at her bedside holding her hand, she told us about the angel.

She was unable to open her eyes and wasn't really able to communicate. I leant my face close to her ear and said very softly, "Hi, Nan. It's me. How are you today? Are you OK?"

She instantly broke into a big smile.

"Oh yes," she whispered, her eyes closed.

"The angel was at the window ... Oh, such a beautiful face," Nan whispered, nodding ever so slightly with each word, still smiling.

"Angel, Nan. What angel?" I said gently, looking across at my Mum and my Great Aunt. They had also been in the room, and as they had heard Nan's voice, they were now on their feet, straining to hear what she was saying.

Nan hadn't really spoken much in the last day or two.

"Really, Nan? There was an angel at the window?" I asked her gently.

Smiling again at the mention of it, she whispered, "Yes ... The angel ... such a beautiful face."

Then after a slight pause, Nan spoke again, her eyes still closed: "The angel said, 'Everything is going to be OK.'"

I leant forward even closer to her ear, glancing at my Mum and Great Aunt.

"Really, Nan? The angel said everything is going to be OK?" I whispered, fighting back the tears.

"Oh ... yes ... everything is going to be OK," she whispered, grinning as she spoke each word softly and clearly.

With that, my Mum, Great Aunt and I melted into tears. We had been huddled together, not wanting to miss a word Nan said.

Those were the last few words Nan spoke before she passed away very peacefully, a few days later.

I will remember them for the rest of my life.

Those four months were the hardest and most painful four months the children and I have ever endured. Up until now we have never experienced watching a loved one decline so rapidly. It was utterly awful. Nothing could have prepared us for it, nothing at all.

A few weeks later, in May 2013, I sat in the front row of the little church at the crematorium. I sat next to my children, Mum, Dad and one of my very best friends. I was really nervous. As my name was called, I stood up and stepped forward. My hands were shaking and my mouth dry.

I gripped my piece of paper and stepped into the little pulpit to face the crowd. When I looked up, the first thing I noticed was that the room was full of people. Every seat was taken.

My voice quivered as I began to speak. I read out a shortened version of my letter to Nan.

After the service was finished, we stepped outside into the fresh air. As we walked to see the flowers, I turned around to be greeted by my ex-husband, my brother-in-law and my mother-in-law.

My ex-husband reached out to give me a hug and I hugged him so tight. I was so glad he was there. Nan, after all, had been his Nan too. He was her grandson. She had been his Nan for twenty years and he loved her too.

In those last four months my ex-husband had visited my Nan a couple of times. That had been the first time he had visited her since we separated in March 2010. She had seen him at the usual family events over recent years at my house, but this was different. He had visited her himself. She had been so pleased to see him.

When I stepped back, I gave my brother-in-law a massive hug too. Then my mother-in-law wrapped her arms around me, giving me the biggest hug ever!

We were all there together: my family and his family. We were *one* family grieving the loss of one of our family members who had meant so much to each of us.

A short while later we attended the wake. I witnessed how powerful unity and love really is.

We all sat together: my children, parents, family, and friends, all sat with my ex-husband and my mother-in-law talking and laughing.

That day changed me.

That was the day that I realised, with full impact, that our families were in unity and their relationship with one another went way beyond me and my ex-husband's relationship. They loved one another with a richness of love that stretched over twenty years.

It was a very sad day, but it was an extremely significant one.

July 2013

New bridges were built that day between my ex-husband and my Dad. So much so, that now it is July 2013 and last week my son mentioned that he, my Dad and my ex-husband are planning to each purchase a season ticket to go and watch football this season! My son is *really* excited about that!

It may not be as it was nearly three and a half years ago, but it is *definitely* going to be a new beginning!

Taking a Brave Step

My Nan was eighty-nine, when she took the brave step, to make her own peace with God.

If you know that you need to make peace with God too, then don't delay. There is hope in God for everything.

If you feel that you want to, then pray the simple prayer opposite with *all your heart,* wherever you are right now:

> Dear Lord Jesus
> Please forgive me for my sins
> I believe that You died on the Cross for me
> Please forgive me for being angry with you, Lord Jesus
> Please forgive me for holding onto un-forgiveness
> I now choose to forgive those who have hurt me
> I ask You, Lord Jesus, to bless them today
> I choose to receive Your forgiveness
> Thank you for forgiving me
> Thank you for loving me unconditionally
> I choose to receive Your love
> Help me to walk in Your love every day
> I invite You, Lord Jesus Christ, to live in my heart
> I give my life to You, Lord Jesus Christ
> Thank you for being my Lord and Saviour
> I now choose to follow You, Lord Jesus Christ.
> In Jesus name, Amen.

I pray that God will pour His abundant blessing into your life today.

God has the answers. He knows *your* needs.

As I type these final few words, I am aware of the time. I am going to meet my ex-husband for lunch in one hour. My eldest daughter, hearing this news a few moments ago whilst in the kitchen, said rather dramatically (laughing with eyebrows raised), "Oh Mum! Any other parent would *not* be meeting up with their ex-husband who left the family! Only *you!* What is *wrong* with you?"

I burst out laughing. So did she.

She turned on her heel, raised her arms in the air and walked into the lounge shaking her head, chuckling at the same time.

The truth was, I hadn't met up with him for a while and it would be a good opportunity to discuss how we would help our two older teenagers with job-hunting, and September course decision-making.

As I searched for my handbag and door keys I was still chuckling to myself. It reminded me of what my son said two days ago. We were sat eating dinner after visiting his art exhibition at school. One minute I was praising him for his artwork, the next he said, "Mum, it was really nice when you hugged Dad at Nanny's funeral."

"Really? What do you mean?" I asked, genuinely surprised by his comment.

"Well, it was just *nice*. You get along really well, Mum, don't you? I mean, you are sort of like you used to be, you know – you and Dad, but *different*, if you know what I mean."

I did know what he meant.

If God had told me the day that my ex-husband left our marriage three years and four months ago, that I would love him for being the Dad of our children, part of our family, *and* that we would be friends … I would never have believed Him. How could that *possibly* happen?

But it has.

The Extra Chocolate

It reminded me of what happened one morning in June 2013, a few weeks ago.

God set me a new challenge.

My ex-husband was looking after the children at my house one particular Friday evening after school. I had wanted to make a special tea for them, so I had gone food shopping the night before. On the Friday morning I set the tea out on the table.

Then as a treat, I picked up four chocolate bar packets: each contained three individual chocolate bars. I took four little squares of plain paper and wrote one of my children's names on each one, along with my ex-husband's name on another. Underneath I added a little cross symbolising a kiss, and using sticky tape, stuck them on top of each chocolate bar packet.

That was all fine until I realised what I had done … I had purchased five packets of chocolate instead of four. I never buy five packets of anything any more; I always now buy four.

I looked at the spare packet of chocolate bars. It made me a little uneasy. I felt God saying I should write my ex-husband's girlfriend's name on it: *the one he had left me for.* "OK," I mumbled under my breath. That was fine too.

I had forgiven her a long time ago.

Then I looked at her name on that little piece of paper. It looked a little odd. It was missing a little cross on it like the others. *Oh dear! What do I do now?*

I thought to myself – '*What is the problem? What am I doing? Why am I worried?*' So I picked the pen up again and added a little cross under her name like all the others. I hid the chocolate bar packet under my ex-husband's on the table amongst the other food items.

When I walked through the door later that evening, I was greeted with, "Mum, when Dad picked up his packet of chocolate, and saw one underneath with his girlfriend's name on … he stood there and said "Oh …""

I don't know who was more surprised, my ex-husband, or my children.

That was *my* brave step. There have been many, but this was a significantly brave step. It was so incredibly unlike me, that I had almost stuck her name on that packet of chocolate so fast before I had the hint of an opportunity to change my mind.

I remember that particular morning so well. I had felt like singing all day.

Forgiveness is only one part. Actually *walking* in love and forgiveness and *showing* love and forgiveness to the people who have hurt you really badly – that takes one *giant* leap!

Later that evening, I received a text from my ex-husband saying, "Thanks for the tea and thanks for the chocolate."

I am so grateful to God for showing me how to walk in love, His way.

The power of forgiveness is incredible!

My eyes are fixed on Jesus ...

What about *you*?

The Eagle

The Front Cover

As I looked at the large canvas painting in my hands, faith rose into my heart.

I knew the moment I saw it being painted, that it was the picture I had been searching for, for months.

The eagle looked to me as if it was soaring through the fierce storm, wing tips skimming the surface of the raging waves of the sea.

There was no bandage on its wings – it was flying free, despite the turbulent waters beneath.

In March 2010, a few weeks after my husband moved out, God gave me a picture:

The picture was of an eagle flying high in the sky – high above mountains.
One of its wings was bandaged.

Then I felt the Lord say to me, "One day the bandage will be removed and you will be able to fly."

I didn't know when that bandage was going to be removed, but I had faith that it would – one day.

As I now hold the painting in my hands, four years and two months later, I clearly see it – *healing*.

I have held onto God's promise that one day that bandage would be removed and my heart would be *whole* again.

Free from grief and pain. *Free* from the devastating effects of abandonment, rejection and being left unloved.

I can say with absolute certainty that I know that I am healed. God has completely healed my heart and set me...

Free.

My heartfelt thanks, to my friend Jenny Whitfield for painting the front cover.

Jenny I love your work, you are the most amazing artist. Love Toni x

Further Information

In memory of my Nan:

Thank you so very much for purchasing this book.

In memory of my beloved Nan and in the hope that this book Crumble or Stand: *The Power of Forgiveness* makes a profit, I will be donating 10% of the profits to Cancer Research.

Thank you

Toni x

For further copies of this book, please visit:

www.lulu.com/wordsbydesign

For any queries regarding this book please email:

admin@toniannbooks.co.uk

A workbook is available that compliments this book.

From the Preface to *Crumble or Stand: The Workbook*:

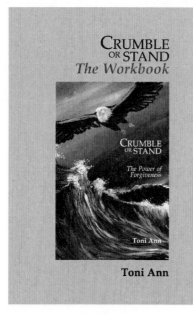

Toni Ann

This is a ten-session workbook offering you key elements from my original book, with the aim to give you ideas of how you can try to put some of its principles into practice in your own life. This can be used on your own; with a small group; or with someone you trust.

Walking in love and forgiveness is not an easy task, especially towards those who have hurt us, but it *is* possible and there are numerous rewards.

When my husband walked out of our marriage, our family, our front door - in pursuit of another woman, it left me feeling abandoned, rejected and alone.

Despite the many months of harrowing turmoil and pain, God showed me step by step, day by day how to love the unlovable and how to forgive the unforgivable.

I have emerged a much stronger person, with my self-respect in-tact and a new-found confidence.

Maybe you have not found yourself in the same situation as I was in. Maybe you can identify with the feelings of loss, abandonment, rejection and grief, for your own reasons.

However you decide to use this workbook, I hope that by the end, you will discover that you *can* stand!

Available to order from www.lulu.com/wordsbydesign